Creating Entrepreneurial Universities: Organizational Pathways of Transformation

ISSUES IN HIGHER EDUCATION
Series Editor: GUY NEAVE, International Association of Universities, Paris, France

Other titles in the series include

Creating Entrepreneurial Universities: Organizational Pathways of Transformation

Burton R. Clark

IAU
PRESS

Published for the IAU Press
PERGAMON

UK   Elsevier Science Ltd, The Boulevard, Langford Lane, Kidlington, Oxford OX5 1GB, U.K.

USA   Elsevier Science Regional Sales Office, 655 Avenue of the Americas, New York, NY 10010, U.S.A.

JAPAN   Elsevier Science Japan, Higashi Azabu 1-chome Building 4F, 1-9-15, Higashi Azabu, Minato-ku, Tokyo 106, Japan

---

First edition 1998
Second impression 1998

Library of Congress Cataloging-in-Publication Data
A catalog record for this book is available from the
Library of Congress

British Library Cataloguing in Publication Data
A catalogue record for this book is available from the
British Library.

ISBN 0 08 0433421 (Hard-back edition)
     0 08 0433545 (Limp-bound edition)

The opinions expressed by the author do not engage the responsibility of the IAU nor of its Administrative Board

Printed in Great Britain by Biddles Ltd, Guildford, Surrey.

The IAU

The International Association of Universities (IAU), founded in 1950, is a worldwide organization with member institutions in over 120 countries, which cooperates with a vast network of international, regional and national bodies. Its permanent Secretariat, the International Universities Bureau, is located at UNESCO, Paris, and provides a wide variety of services to Member Institutions and to the international higher education community at large.

Activities and Services

* IAU–UNESCO Information Centre on Higher Education
* International Information Networks
* Meetings and seminars
* Research and studies
* Promotion of academic mobility and cooperation
* Credential evaluation
* Consultancy
* Exchange of publications and materials

Publications

* International Handbook of Universities
* World List of Universities
* Issues in Higher Education (monographs)
* Papers and Reports
* Higher Education Policy (quarterly)
* IAU Bulletin (bimonthly)

*To my wife, Adele, for a half-century
of loving lucidity*

Introduction to Issues in Higher Education

For the past quarter century, higher education has been high on the agenda of governments and central to the fortune of nations. Similarly, this same period has seen quite massive changes in direction, in the complexity of systems, in the underlying rationale which has accompanied such changes and in the sheer size of the enterprise in terms of students, staff and budgets, not to mention social and economic purpose. It is not surprising then that the study of higher education itself has broadened and now encompasses some 20 different disciplines, ranging from Anthropology through to Women's Studies, each with its own particular paradigms, methodologies and perspectives.

Against this background, the comparative analysis of higher education policy which has always occupied a crucial place in understanding the contextual setting of reform in individual countries, has acquired a new significance as the pace of "internationalization" itself quickens. There are many reasons why this should be so: the creation of new economic blocs and, in the case of Europe, the gradual emergence of a trans-national policy for higher education across the EC countries; the triumph of one industrial ethnic and the collapse of another, the rise of new economies in Asia, etc. The breakdown of a seemingly established order has ushered in a renewed interest in other models of higher education and in how other nations are going about tackling often similar issues though in different ways. This series has the purpose of examining issues and testing theories in the field of higher education policy which are of current and practical concern to its main constituencies—national and institutional leadership, administrators, teachers, those researching in this domain and students. As a series, it will focus on both advanced industrial and also on developing systems of higher education.

Issues in Higher Education will be resolutely comparative in its approach and will actively encourage original studies which are firmly based around an international perspective. Individual volumes will be based on a minimum of two different countries so as to bring out the variations occurring in a given problématique. Every encouragement will be given to the drawing of clear and explicit comparisons between the higher education systems covered.

As the editor, I wish to thank the members of the Educational Advisory Board for their part in developing this series. They are:

Jose Joaquim Brunner, *FLACSO (Latin American Faculty for Social Sciences), Santiago, Chile*

Burton R. Clark, *Emeritus Professor, Graduate School of Education, University of California, Los Angeles*

Dan Levy, *Professor of Educational Administration and Policy Studies, State University of New York, Albany, USA*

Lynn Meek, *Department of Public Administration and Studies in Higher Education, University of New England Armidale, New South Wales, Australia*

Hassan Mekouar, *University Mohammed V, Morocco*

Keto Mshigeni, *The Graduate School, University of Dar-es-Salaam, Tanzania*

Agilakpa Sawyerr, *African Association of Universities, Accra, Ghana*

Ulrich Teichler, *Director of the Research Centre for Higher Education and the Labour Market, University of Kassel, Germany*

Morikazu Ushiogi, *Department of Higher Education, Nagoya University, Japan*

Frans van Vught, *Rector, University of Twente, Enschede, The Netherlands*

Fang Min Wei, *Institute of Higher Education at Beijing University, The People's Republic of China*

GUY NEAVE
International Association of Universities
Paris, France

Contents

List of Tables

Acknowledgments

During my visits to the five European universities that took part in this study, from late 1994 to the end of 1996, I was warmly received by faculty, administrative officials, lay board members, students, and staff. I am indeed indebted to several hundred individuals at these institutions, here unnamed, for their cordial reception and willingness to discuss with an inquiring stranger the development and character of their universities. At each place a few individuals led the way in arranging cooperation, scheduling visits, and critically reviewing penultimate drafts of specific chapters. I wish to thank particularly Michael Shattock, registrar, and two of his assistants, Jennifer Nutkins and Paul Anderson of the University of Warwick; Peter Maassen and Frans A. Van Vught, then associate director and director of the Center for Higher Education Policy Studies (CHEPS), University of Twente; Peter West, university secretary, and his secretary Fiona Murchie, University of Strathclyde; Roger Johansson, planning officer, and his assistant, Helen Strömberg, Chalmers Institute of Technology; and Seppo Höltta, planning officer, University of Joensuu. Ben Jongbloed, CHEPS researcher, also contributed a helpful critical review of the Twente draft.

These colleagues, with their thoughtful and caring assistance, afforded me the opportunity to range across the institutions to talk, observe, and gather information at will; they also often extended invitations to lectures, concerts, and special dinners. I spent many graceful days at these universities; the five developmental narratives offered in this volume probably reveal, more than I intended, the fact that I grew to like and to admire each of these institutions. I have always thought that universities are remarkable organizations, and when they are able to manage themselves in a reasonably integrated fashion, they become more so.

Two American foundations funded the study. The Mellon Foundation and the Spencer Education Foundation helped me to get started with small grants in 1994. Mellon then provided a major grant in early 1995 for two years of fieldwork in Europe, manuscript preparation, and the presentation of papers at international conferences. I am particularly indebted to Harriet Zuckerman, vice-president of the foundation, for her faith in the value of this inquiry into international higher education.

I am grateful to the UCLA Graduate School of Education and Information Studies for retaining me on its faculty – a half-dozen years after formal retirement – and for providing me with office and support services. Patricia Smith, my long-standing administrative assistant, processed more drafts of the chapters of this book than she and I care to remember. My wife, Adele Clark, edited the entire manuscript with a sharp eye for soggy expression: if the book reads clearly she deserves the credit. For factual and interpretive errors, I am solely responsible.

I also wish to express my gratitude to Guy Neave, research director of the International Association of Universities and editor of the series in which this book appears, for his engaging friendship and colleagueship sustained over many years. He has made the study of higher education in all its comparative and international aspects a delight. He and a few other senior colleagues – Frans A. Van Vught (The Netherlands), Ulrich Teichler (Germany), and Maurice Kogan (Britain) in particular – have made the Europe-based Consortium of Higher Education Researchers (CHER), over the course of a decade, the centerpiece of an "invisible college" that now extends virtually around the world. I have been fortunate to have been included.

Burton R. Clark
Santa Monica, California
July, 1997

Introduction

The universities of the world have entered a time of disquieting turmoil that has no end in sight. As the difficulties of universities mounted across the globe during the last quarter of the twentieth century, higher education lost whatever steady state it may have once possessed. Since expanding demands will not relent, conditions of constancy cannot return. The expansion of student demand continues virtually without end. More students and more different types of students of all ages appear at the doors of universities and colleges to be diversely and repeatedly educated in a growing array of subjects and programs of educational renewal. Knowledge-based enterprises in the economy and society create an expanding and rapidly changing professional labor market for which universities are expected to provide competent graduates. Governments expect universities to do much more for society in solving economic and social problems, but at the same time they back and fill in their financial support and become unreliable patrons. Most important, the research base of the university world rapidly creates new knowledge and technique, steadily increasing specialties and stretching the range of disciplinary and interdisciplinary fields. Universities are based on knowledge, but no university or set of universities can stop or even seriously slow its international growth. Caught in the swell of knowledge production, even the richest institutions find full coverage of old and new fields beyond their capability.

Pushed and pulled by enlarging, interacting streams of demand, universities are pressured to change their curricula, alter their faculties, and modernize their increasingly expensive physical plant and equipment – and to do so more rapidly than ever. Some traditional fields of study are bypassed, others fall into disarray. With the humanities now highly vulnerable, critics contend that universities do not know where they are going, even that they have lost their souls. We can be sure that if universities are not to lose their bearings while exploring new possibilities and adding new activities, they will need not only to maintain but also to reconstitute many of their traditional offerings.

With complexity and uncertainty now endemic, no one knows with any degree of confidence what the twenty-first century holds in store for universities. How then to proceed? One answer stands out: step by step, learn by experimenting. We need widespread experimentation that tests ways to move into the future. We need particularly to learn from efforts to innovate in the overall character of universities.

This study reports research on a handful of universities in Europe that made a valiant effort in the 1980s and early 1990s to become more enterprising, even aggressively entrepreneurial. In traditional European settings, enterprising universities are places that actively seek to move away from close governmental regulation and sector standardization. They search for special organizational identities; they risk being different; they take chances in "the market." They adhere to the belief that the risks of experimental change in the character of universities should be chosen over the risks of simply maintaining traditional forms and practices.

To identify universities for this study I informally canvassed European colleagues active in studying higher education for their nomination of institutions that had been involved in self-instituting efforts to change their general character for eight to ten years or more. I viewed a decade as a minimal period of time for serious change in the ways of a university to be instituted and worked out. Therefore I would track developments from the early-to-mid 1980s to the mid-1990s. With this time-span in mind, several major European systems seemed to have little to offer; serious transforming efforts in even a few of their institutions were not attempted until well into the 1990s. The universities of France, Germany, and Italy were dropped from the network of possibilities. When I turned to Britain and the small nations of northern Europe, the University of Warwick in England and the University of Twente in The Netherlands – frequently mentioned by others – became the first two choices for investigation. I then subsequently became persuaded through nominations and documents that the University of Strathclyde would be an interesting case to explore in Scotland; that Chalmers University of Technology in Sweden must have experienced a special type of development that led up to its major 1994 "privatizing" change in status; and that the University of Joensuu had clearly set out on a different pathway in the mid- and late-1980s when it became a pilot institution for a basic kind of organizational change in Finland. Under limitations of time, energy, and research budget, five cases in such varied national settings were deemed sufficient.

The research consisted of two rounds of one-to-two-week visits during late 1994, 1995, and 1996. My research method was simple. During each visit I engaged in about a dozen taped interviews with faculty, administrators, and students, each lasting one to two hours. I also foraged for documents to review and to carry away (universities in The Netherlands, Sweden, and Finland publish major documents in English); sat in on a few meetings, where possible; and looked around at what was going on in the offices, classrooms, laboratories, corridors, and pathways of the campus. The analysis of gathered materials then depended on several rounds of data reduction to extract the information needed for brief institutional narratives and to provide the empirical content of emerging concepts. Throughout the book I have quoted extensively from both documents and interviews; the quoted material that appears without documentary reference has been taken from the interviews, without – in almost all cases – reference made to an individual.

Since I wanted to determine how each university had gone about changing its organization and practices, I had to pursue peculiarities and come to terms with unique configurations. But I wanted particularly to identify common pathways of transformation, if they existed, that might compose rudiments of middle range conceptualization. Such elements were identified halfway through the research and then pursued intensely in the second round of visits. Thus, the concepts that came to rule the study largely emerged from the research and then were used to orient the future work. My mode of reasoning was primarily inductive, largely bottom-up from analyzed experiences. It was more from "practice" to "theory" than the other way around. In the domain of universities, theory cannot aim for exacting one-size-fits-all. But we can aim for explanatory categories that stretch across a set of institutions, which, at the same time, do not do violence to institutional peculiarities. We can devise covering categories that explain a plurality of cases without distorting their uniquenesses. Such "relevant theorizing" can stand us in good stead in understanding university change.

I have organized this book in a special way that combines conceptual analysis with institutional stories. To clarify and highlight the concepts, they are introduced first: chapter one specifies the common elements extracted from the research. The elements are then used to provide a coherent structure around which to spin out the institutional stories – the case studies – presented in chapters two to six. The institutional accounts serve several essential purposes. They hold together empirical materials on each university; they report historical detail and bring forth the unique composite way by which any one organization in any one setting develops. Most important, they allow us to see the primary elements develop over time and interact. The highlighted pathways lose any claim to fixed sequence or exclusivity. They vary in primacy of appearance; as they link and blend, they support one another. The accounts often take us beyond common notions that "leadership" and "mission" always come first in the transformation of universities.

In the middle institutional chapters, where I weave the elements into the case studies from which they were derived, I have adapted a particular prose style as a useful compromise between generalizing concepts and institutional individuality. The common elements structure each chapter but they are not set off as separate headings. They are blended into the historical narratives and are simply italicized as they repeatedly appear in streams of development. We thereby simultaneously stay focused on five pathways of development and put them in their place in each institution, all the better to see them at work in the swirling reality of organizational action and change. We then see the elements interacting with one another *and* with special features of each institution not highlighted but which should not be overlooked. We see each element develop over time during ten to fifteen years of organizational effort: for example, the financial base steadily becomes more diversified; an institutional "idea" becomes elaborated into a set of beliefs that become a new culture.

After an institutional pursuit that discursively moves from England to Holland to Scotland to Sweden and then to Finland in Part II, the final chapter returns to the organizing concepts, now placed within a larger framework for thinking about university transformation. A primary question is confronted: are universities now under increasing pressure to reshape themselves? If so, why? At root, what is so threatening that it virtually impels their transformation toward a lasting entrepreneurial posture? I suggest that a thesis of imbalance offers a parsimonious answer. The university-environment relationship is characterized by a deepening asymmetry between environmental demand and institutional capacity to respond. The imbalance creates a problem of institutional insufficiency. So much is now demanded of universities that traditional ways prove inadequate. Universities require not only an enlarged capacity to respond to changes in the external worlds of government, business, and civic life but also a better honed ability to bring demands under control by greater focus in institutional character. Strongly needed is an overall capacity to respond flexibly and selectively to changes taking place within the knowledge domains of the university world itself.

University change in Europe at the end of the twentieth century, and arguably elsewhere in the world, centers on the development of self-regulating universities, places that actively seek out stronger means to become and remain competent societal institutions. The specific elements identified in this study serve as such means. Relatively concrete, the operational pathways developed here are more tangible to the touch than the grand rhetorics that flow readily in and around universities in ambiguous terms of liberal and professional education, accountability and assessment, bureaucracy and community, state and market. Broad interests in purpose and implementation are brought down to specific categories of university organization. We follow the trail of the simple maxim that universities change their character as they change specific ways in which they operate.

The five universities analyzed in this study can be seen as experiments in the construction of change. They are not alone: other universities have also been actively working on significant change in their character and we may expect more to engage in such efforts. System officials, university administrators, faculty, students, outside concerned observers, all need a better working knowledge of options and limitations. University transformation has moved to the top of the agenda in the understanding of modern higher education.

Part I

Pathways of Transformation

1

Entrepreneurial Pathways of University Transformation

Explanation of how five universities in five different European settings went about changing their character to become more adaptive institutions requires that we acknowledge the individuality of institutional development. Accordingly, the five central chapters organize descriptive materials as case studies in which an understanding of each institution's setting and historic character is seen as necessary for understanding whatever transformation has taken place or is in process. Each account includes what is significantly unique and peculiar and the role played by particular individuals. The integrated case reports assert the special character of each of the universities that compose the empirical base of the study. They portray singular local flavor.

But, as stressed in the introduction, the separate stories are not the commanding interest. Common elements found in the case studies allow us to push beyond unique histories. Together they strongly suggest how universities that have willed themselves to change differ systematically from those that remain entirely encapsulated in a traditional mode. This chapter briefly sets forth these major features.

The Concept of Entrepreneurial University

"Entrepreneurial" is taken in this study as a characteristic of social systems; that is, of entire universities and their internal departments, research centers, faculties, and schools. The concept carries the overtones of "enterprise" – a willful effort in institution-building that requires much special activity and energy. Taking risks when initiating new practices whose outcome is in doubt is a major factor. An entrepreneurial university, on its own, actively seeks to innovate in how it goes about its business. It seeks to work out a substantial shift in organizational character so as to arrive at a more promising posture for the future. Entrepreneurial universities seek to become "stand-up" universities that are significant actors on their own terms. Institutional entrepreneurship can be seen as both process and outcome.

Throughout much of the two years and more of the research, the two terms "entrepreneurial" and "innovative" were used as loosely synonymous. The concept of "innovative university" has much appeal. Gentler in overtone, it also casts a wider net. It avoids the negative connotations that many academics attach to individual entrepreneurs as aggressive business-oriented people seeking to maximize profit. When the institutions in this study, together with a few other universities, established a new all-Europe voluntary association of highly limited membership in 1996, they had good reason to name it "The European Consortium of Innovative Universities." But I have chosen "entrepreneurial" over "innovative" as the organizing conception for this book because it points more powerfully to deliberate local effort, to actions that lead to change in organizational posture. Under its banner I can more appropriately group some processes by which modern universities measurably change themselves.

University transformation, for the most part, is not accidental or incidental. It does not happen because several innovative programs are established here and there within a university: the new approaches can be readily sealed off as minor enclaves. It does not happen because a solitary entrepreneur captures power and runs everything from the top-down: such cases are exceptions to the rule. Universities are too bottom-heavy, too resistant from the bottom-up, for tycoons to dominate very long. Rather, transformation occurs when a number of individuals come together in university basic units and across a university over a number of years to change, by means of organized initiative, how the institution is structured and oriented. *Collective* entrepreneurial action at these levels is at the heart of the transformation phenomenon. Acting from on-high, national and state systems of higher education are blunt instruments of significant change; acting from below, individual faculty members or administrators are limited in what they can do. But groups, large and small – central and departmental – of faculty and administrators (and sometimes students!) can fashion new structures, processes, and orientations whereby a university becomes biased toward adaptive change. Academic groups can also help insure that *academic* values will guide transformation, a point that will appear repeatedly in the institutional narratives. Effective collective entrepreneurship does not carry a university beyond the boundaries of academic legitimacy, setting off a down-market cycle of reputation, resources, and development. Rather, it can provide resources and infrastructures that build capability beyond what a university would otherwise have, thereby allowing it to subsidize and enact an up-market climb in quality and reputation.

A formal grant of autonomy from patron to institution does not guarantee active self-determination; autonomous universities may be passive institutions. They may live for the past rather than look to the future. They may be satisfied with what they have become and do not wish for more. By informal agreement they may have decided to move in lockstep with counterpart institutions in their region or country, together to sink or swim. They are then biased toward standing still. Autonomous universities become active institutions when they decide they must explore and experiment with changes in how they are composed and how they react to internal and external demands. They sense that in fast-moving times the prudent course of action is to be out in front, shaping the impact of demands made upon them, steering instead of drifting. It is then that they need new organizational elements that together characterize the entrepreneurial university.

Pathways of Transformation

How do universities, by means of entrepreneurial action, go about transforming themselves? Five elements constitute an irreducible minimum: a strengthened steering core; an expanded developmental periphery; a diversified funding base; a stimulated academic heartland; and an integrated entrepreneurial culture.

The strengthened steering core

Traditional European universities have long exhibited a notoriously weak capacity to steer themselves. As their complexity has increased and the pace of change accelerated, that weakness has become more debilitating, deepening the need for a greater managerial capacity. Unambitious universities can ignore this need and drift with the tides of traditional patronage. Universities that serve as flagships or elite institutions in their own national or state systems of higher education can ignore the lack of steering capacity longer than others and can continue to depend upon their outstanding reputation and political clout for guaranteed resources and competitive status. But ambitious universities, and universities concerned about their marginality, and even their survivability, cannot depend on old habits of weak steering. They need to become quicker, more flexible, and especially more focused in reactions to expanding and changing demands. They need a more organized way to refashion their programmatic capabilities. A strengthened steering core becomes a necessity. As we shall see, that core can take quite different shapes. But it must embrace central managerial groups *and* academic departments. It must operationally reconcile new managerial values with traditional academic ones.

The expanded developmental periphery

Enterprising universities exhibit a growth of units that, more readily than traditional academic departments, reach across old university boundaries to link up with outside organizations and groups. In one form these units are professionalized outreach offices that work on knowledge transfer, industrial contact, intellectual property development, continuing education, fundraising, and even alumni affairs. In another larger, and more basic, form they are interdisciplinary project-oriented research centers that grow up alongside departments as a second major way to group academic work. Academic departments based on disciplinary fields of knowledge will go on being important: their disciplinary competence is essential, too valuable to throw away, and they have much power with which to protect their own domains. But the departments alone cannot do all the things that universities now need to do. Outward-reaching research centers express nondisciplinary definitions of problems. They bring into the university the project orientation of outsiders who are attempting to solve serious practical problems critical in economic and social development. They have a certain flexibility in that they are relatively easy to initiate and to disband. Constructed to cross old boundaries, the centers mediate between departments and the outside world.

If a university's trade with external groups is to continue to evolve, its infrastructure must keep pace. Anxious to find better tools for coping with societal demands, entrepreneurial universities take the risk of promoting an entire new periphery of nontraditional units. As we shall see, substantial organizational creativity is involved.

The diversified funding base

To fashion a new change-oriented character, a university generally requires greater financial resources: it particularly needs discretionary funds. Widening the financial base becomes essential, since virtually everywhere mainline institutional support from government, as a share of total budget, is on the wane. Enterprising universities recognize this trend and turn it to advantage. They step up their efforts to raise money from a second major source, research councils, by more vigorously competing for grants and contracts. They set out to construct a widening and deepening portfolio of third-stream income sources that stretch from industrial firms, local governments, and philanthropic foundations, to royalty income from intellectual property, earned income from campus services, student fees, and alumni fundraising. Third-stream sources represent true financial diversification. They are especially valuable in providing discretionary money, beyond overhead charges and top-sliced sums extracted from research grants.

In the process of increasing income from the second and third streams, entrepreneurial universities learn faster than nonentrepreneurial counterparts that money from many sources enhances the opportunity to make significant moves without waiting for systemwide enactments that come slowly, with standardizing rules attached. They accept and promote the maxim offered by two American observers as long ago as the early 1960s: "a workable twentieth century definition of institutional autonomy [is] the absence of dependence upon a single or narrow base of support." (Babbidge and Rosenzweig, 1962, p. 158)

The stimulated academic heartland

When an enterprising university evolves a stronger steering core, *and* develops an outreach structure, *and* diversifies its income streams, its heartland is still found in the traditional academic departments formed around disciplines, new and old, and some interdisciplinary fields of study. Spread across the operating base of the university as sites of research and particularly of teaching, the basic units, and their more encompassing multidepartment faculties, continue to be the places where most academic work is done. Whether they accept or oppose a significant transformation is critical. It is here in the many units of the heartland that promoted changes and innovative steps are most likely to fail. If the basic units oppose or ignore would-be innovations, the life of the institution proceeds largely as before. For change to take hold, one department and faculty after another needs itself to become an entrepreneurial unit, reaching more strongly to the outside with new programs and relationships and promoting third-stream income. Their members need to participate in central steering groups. They need to accept that individuals as well as collegial groups will have stronger authority in a managerial line that stretches from central officials to heads of departments and research centers.

The heartland is where traditional academic values are most firmly rooted. The required blending of those values with the newer managerial points of view must, for the most part, be worked out at that level. In the entrepreneurial university, the heartland accepts a modified belief system.

The integrated entrepreneurial culture

Enterprising universities, much as firms in the high tech industry, develop a work culture that embraces change. That new culture may start out as a relatively simple institutional idea about change that later becomes elaborated into a set of beliefs which, if diffused in the heartland, becomes a universitywide culture. Strong cultures are rooted in strong practices. As ideas and practices interact, the cultural or symbolic side of the university becomes particularly important in cultivating institutional identity and distinctive reputation.

In the transformation of universities, values or beliefs may lead or follow the development of the other elements. We shall see them in cycles of interaction, themselves developing over time. Organizational values ought not be treated independently of the structures and procedures through which they are expressed. An *institutional* perspective is required. The first four of our five elements are means by which transforming beliefs are made operative.

*   *   *   *

I wish to stress again that the conceptualization of these five common transforming elements developed in the course of research. Initial categories used during the first year of the study were broad and open-ended. In interviews I began with the personal background of the respondent and then moved on to five major topics: the overall character of the university; the nature of leadership, past and present; the relationship between the administration and the faculty; the bases of financial support; and the shape of research and advanced training – a category much on my mind from the focus of a prior project. (Clark, 1995a) The exploratory categories were set out in a paper delivered at an international conference in the summer of 1994; it appeared later in an article on "leadership and innovation in universities." (Clark, 1995b) After the first visits to four of the institutions – Warwick, Twente, Strathclyde, and Chalmers – I attempted "midstream" to develop more pointed and useful categories. They were reported in a second conference paper and follow-on article as a one-year progress report. (Clark, 1996) I used the newly created common elements during the second round of field visits in 1996 both to clarify their conceptualization and empirical reach, and to determine if additional categories were needed. The five features offered a welcomed simplicity among the many that might have been discussed. Here presented in particularly simplified form, they become more elaborated when they are plunged into the complex realities of individual university development.

Without doubt, significant innovation in the character of a university means that some core tasks and some deep structures are altered to the point where the long-term course of the organization is changed. Such transforming work must be done locally, in the university itself. It must extend over years that often become decades. The sustained work calls for collective action leading to new practices and beliefs, steps that are entrepreneurial in character, with much risk-taking and flexible adjustment along the way. When traditional habits are not enough, universities need to develop *an entrepreneurial response*. In the institutional case studies that follow, we will see that response, variously fashioned in detail, composed of the features that are here identified as basic elements of transformation.

Part II:

Case Studies of European

Innovative Universities

Part II.

Case Studies of European Research Active Innovative Universities

2

The Warwick Way: Transformation in an English Research University

The University of Warwick in the United Kingdom is a good place to begin a case-by-case analysis of entrepreneurial action in European universities. By the mid-1990s the university had acquired a strong reputation as a distinctive entrepreneurial place, a model for Europe and arguably other parts of the world. Whatever Warwick had done to shape its character had been accomplished in only three decades, since its establishment in the mid-1960s: a short time in the life of a university. Decisive character-forming steps on which we will concentrate were initiated in the early 1980s, establishing the following decade and a half as the time when critical pathways of transformation were devised and institutionalized. But the earlier years are not unimportant; certain character-shaping habits were established then. From the outset the Warwick road was not easy, and there were major bumps along the way. In the late 1960s, only a few years after it opened, for example, the university became a target of radical discontent and student disruption, producing for a time a public image that brought much criticism from both the Left and the Right. We find no simple story of initial clear mission, sustained sponsorship, and linear progress. Warwick is a study of struggle and triumph over serious obstacles – a study in self-determination.

Early Imprints

Much was upbeat in British higher education in the 1950s and early 1960s, the last time that resources and governmental attitude would give rise to a general optimism in leading academic circles that well-guided gentle expansion could add a few more institutions and a few more students to extend the virtues of an elite, high-quality university system. Britain had long been careful about adding to the small list of recognized universities. Institutions developed into universities by first serving for an extended period as a college supervised by an old established place. When aspiring institutions were thought to be finally up to the mark of national standards, they were "upgraded" to full university standing. But in the optimism of the 1950s and with looming system expansion, the idea that perhaps some new universities ought to be allowed to develop from scratch gradually gained favor. The group of supplicants that worked their way through an elaborate political and educational process to the top of the "batting order" became seven in number, known as the Seven Sisters: Sussex, York, Lancaster, Essex, East Anglia, Kent, and Warwick. The seven became "a unique phenomenon: the only universities since London and Durham in the 1830s to leap into existence fully armed, with the whole panoply of first and postgraduate degrees, curricula designed from scratch, in brand new buildings on virgin sites, able to create themselves in whatever image they chose." (Perkin, 1991, p. 295) All were established outside cities, with student residencies, and became known as "green-fields universities."

Given this special opportunity, the New Universities (as they became known) could not only serve the general expansion of British higher education but also test anew the possibilities and virtues of somewhat isolated communities in which faculty and students would interact in small-group teaching and share campus pathways. "Interdisciplinarity" was much discussed in Britain and continental Europe at the time. Expectations were widespread in the University Grants Committee (UGC), the operational patron of the new universities, and in the planning boards established at the universities that the new institutions should give new life to general education for undergraduates: cross-disciplinary subjects organized by broad internal "schools" would replace, or triumph over, narrower departments. Small size would help. Although ambitious to grow, each held to about 3,000 students over the first decade. The University of Sussex, an early leader among the Seven Sisters, underway in 1961 and strongly led by John Fulton and Asa Briggs, took to a pattern of schools. As put by Briggs in a later reflection: "There was only one shared idea on paper which was there when we started our discussion in 1961. That was that we would get rid of departments altogether at Sussex and have 'schools' in their place." (Briggs, 1991, p. 321) The idea, or vision, was not to just "assemble a collection of distinguished academics and leave them to get on with it as individuals," but to stress "active teams." (p. 320)

But as Briggs also noted: "there was a different way of conceiving of a new university, best represented, I believe, at Warwick. Bring professors in and leave them free to get on with it." (p. 324) Not that this approach had clear sailing at Warwick. The inclinations of the UGC were well-known; the university's initial planning board was very interested in the schools concept; the strong first vice-chancellor, Jack Butterworth (1961–1985) was sympathetic to this approach. Local business and union leaders were also involved in early discussions, some as lay members of the planning board, and sought a "relevant" university. (Shattock, 1994b) But Butterworth was first of all committed to academic excellence and was willing to get good people and turn them loose in their specialties. He assembled ten foundation professors in eight subjects to constitute the leading staff on opening day in the fall of 1965.

Among the Seven Sisters, Warwick was the least given to overall planning. As put by A. Phillips Griffiths, initial Professor of Philosophy, in a 25-year retrospective:

> The approaches of the New Universities were very different. Essex's plan arose from a quite different vision from that of Sussex; and these again were quite different from the more departmentally oriented universities. What attracted me about Warwick was not that it had a better, more appealing plan; it was that Warwick hadn't got a plan at all. (Griffiths, 1991, p. 335)

There was "only a universal agreement that a university should aim at excellence." (p. 336) Schools were tried, for example, a School of Literature and a School of Historical Studies (the latter threw french and philosophy together with history!), "but there had also to be some kind of structure related to what was actually going on: so we found that, in addition to Schools, 'Subjects' were referred to in official minutes. . . Each subject had a head, and its own budget." The subjects "became called what they usually are: departments. . . " (p. 339) Schools gradually disappeared. As happens in organizations generally, what was actually going on brought organizational structure in line or ignored it.

Griffiths also noted that the New Universities attracted staff with new ideas that had been frequently stifled in the older institutions. Not wanting to dictate to or impose on one another, "they were perforce involved in a conspiracy of tolerance, a practical libertarian academic contract. . . " (p. 342) And with the new faculty there came "an enthusiasm for research," which led virtually from the beginning, throughout the New Universities, to "a higher proportion of postgraduate [graduate] students." (Thompson, Sir Michael, 1991, p. 346) The UGC, to stress teaching and undergraduate education, wanted the universities to give research a low priority. But this was not to be. The New Universities would not become like "the small American undergraduate colleges which supply the major universities with postgraduate students." (p. 349) Instead, teaching and learning would be research-led.

Thus, in its first decade, Warwick essentially laid down a discipline-centered academic base that would be strong on research. Steadily drifting away from interdisciplinary aspirations and blueprints, the university became a place for research-led departments built by faculty that came on board in disparate fields.

No new plan was offered, but the academic imprint early established was to wear well in later years.

Beyond this academic base the issue of relating to industry arose. Vice-Chancellor Butterworth was close to leading industrialists in the Coventry area and sought to instill a proindustry attitude at the university: it would be a "relevant university" as well as a discipline-led enterprise. It was his idea that a graduate business school was added to the list of new units to be formed around the initial chairs in some eight to ten fields, including engineering science. (University of Warwick, 1991, p. 20) Many public as well as private notables in the region wanted a relevant university – it could help out as an economic resource in its own right and in promoting regional economic development. But the deeply rooted "donnish" anti-industry attitude of British academics was still alive and well in the 1960s and 1970s. Associating with industrialists was problematic. For academic staff, getting on with basic research, finding good students, and building courses of study was enough to do. As assessed by an old-timer in interview, "the academic staff was very loathe to work with industry."

The matter perhaps could have been gradually and gently worked out, but student unrest hit the new university (only a few years old) quite hard in 1969, and ripped open the issue of university-industry connections. A major disruption took place – one of the sharpest to occur in the UK. It involved occupation of the administration building and the riffling of files in which correspondence with industrialists was found. The vice-chancellor and his immediate staff came under severe attack from some faculty as well as militant students, and the episode was capped by an exposé-type book, written in a week and hurriedly published by Penguin, in which Warwick was depicted as a university captured by industry: it was "the business university." E.P. Thompson, the British historian who was then a member of the academic staff, edited the book, and it became known as his *Warwick University Ltd* (1970). For some British academics, especially those on the political Left, the book confirmed the belief that to relate in any way to industry was to be captured by industry, even to be dominated by "capitalism," and that Warwick had more than likely sold out to the devil. The public counterattack from the Right soon saw the university as "the Kremlin on the hill," at least as a newly implanted nest of snobbish dons and of radical students looking for the revolution. There was "a lot of bad press"; much hostility was stirred up on all sides.

But institutional life went on. The vice-chancellor, who "was almost toppled" in 1969–1970, regained his footing and primacy, and the 1970s saw the institution throw off its antibusiness attitudes and assume a much more outward looking focus. The physical plant was substantially enlarged by a second construction phase that filled in the central campus. Income went up from 267,000 pounds in 1965 to nearly 3 million in 1970, further rising to nearly 21 million in 1980. The student body steadily increased in size, from about 450 at the outset to approximately 2,100 in 1970 and 5,200 in 1980.

Academic staff grew from about 60 in 1965 to four times that many in 1970 and to more than 500 in 1980. The university assumed the shape of a somewhat focused medium-size English research university, with disciplinary departments offering work in the physical sciences, life sciences, social sciences, humanities and the arts. To these were added programs in engineering and business. (University of Warwick, 1991, pp. 91–94)

Toward the end of the 1970s, Warwick also began to develop relations with the local community, a role that had been little emphasized while the research focus was being established. A merger of the university and an adjacent college of education in 1978 gave the institution a teacher-education relationship to the local area. Here was a "service job" that could help to fill a long promised commitment to be relevant to local need. A few years later, in the early 1980s, the commitment was extended by the development of extramural or continuing education, very much locally oriented, and the joint sponsorship with local authorities of a science park, features to which we later return. Thus, a second imprint was laid down, a door to community service that later was to be swung wide open.

By the end of its first decade and a half, in 1980, the university had grown internally confident about its quality but was unsure of its national standing. Like the other new universities, it projected a certain attractive quality associated with residential student life. Like the others, its advocates could tell stories about bright students who, given the choice, had selected *it* rather than Oxford or Cambridge, let alone a civic or "redbrick" university. But the institution of that time was also still an immature 15-year old, with adolescent doubts – an institution that had spent much time and effort during the 1970s damping down the negative public image that followed from the student disruption and turning faculty sentiment away from an anti-industry stance. What the university had as major assets were a relatively young, enthusiastic faculty in a department-led research environment coupled with attractive "green-fields" conditions for student life. Financial support was heavily governmental along standard lines used across universities. A growing friendliness to industry and possible outside benefactors had also begun to pay occasional dividends by way of private or local authority support for new buildings and professorial chairs. This particular door to future development was ajar more often than in the other Seven Sisters, favored by location in the West Midlands, the center of the British engineering industry. A good thing too, one can say in hindsight, for the core support of British universities was about to be badly shaken. All were moving into hard times.

University Transformation

Unlike university systems on the Continent, the British system came into existence and developed outside the state; Oxford and Cambridge were established under ecclesiastical patronage and were able to fund themselves from endowments and fees until the twentieth century; the nineteenth-century civic universities were founded by local and private endeavor. (Jones, 1988, Shattock, 1994b) It was not until well into the twentieth century that national government stepped in to pick up the tab and become the principal patron. It provided about one-third of overall funding between the two World Wars; after World War II it took over both recurrent and capital funding to the point of contributing over 90 percent of university budgets. In financial terms, nationalization was about as complete as it could be: reliance on a single patron had become nearly total.

The danger of such dependence became starkly clear in the early 1980s. Financial restraint had already become a serious matter for the universities during the 1970s, but at the end of the decade they could still hope that matters would turn around – that the government would "come to its senses" and fund research and university education on an expanding scale. But the new reality was just the opposite. The Conservative (Thatcher) government came to power in 1979; by 1981 it had effected a first round of heavy budget cuts that across the university system approximated 17 percent over a three-year funding period. The University Grants Committee was permitted to distribute the reductions differentially, and did so over a wide range that extended as high as 20 and 30 percent reductions. Warwick's cut was ten percent, a not inconsequential slice. All the universities were faced with the problem of how to handle their immediate cuts and then especially how to face a future in which mainline funding was likely to continue to falter. This harsh step caused deep shock and far-reaching anger in the academy. A new hostile government was making threats of more to come. What to do? It was here that Warwick began a transforming process.

An *idea* came first. Warwick would cover the ten percent reduction by a "save half, make half policy" – make savings to eliminate half the shortfall and generate new income to cover the other half. Over the next three years it failed in the first part, saving very little, but surprised itself on the earnings part, which led to overall income "12% higher in real terms over what it had been in 1980–81 rather than 10% lower." (Shattock, 1994a, p. 2) A general idea that had been brewing in the registrar's office beginning in 1979 was now given a chance to be born and tested. In the pressure cooker of UK university finance during the early 1980s, it quickly became, for Warwick, a much valued institutional idea.

The idea was sharpened with a strategic decision not to generate new income by "fundraising – "we would not go begging for money" – but to actually earn it. The building of endowment from which interest income would flow, together with an annual passing of the hat among alumni and solicited supporters, was a road not taken. It was seen as too problematic in the English setting at the time. As put later by the much-involved registrar, Michael Shattock: "We had to find ways to generate funding from other sources; we did not see why people or companies would simply give us money so we decided to earn it." (1994a, p.4) Student tuition was largely out of the question, barred by national policy based on a long-standing commitment to subsidize students' academic costs. What Warwick turned to instead was an earning scheme within which various parts of the university – some old, some new – could be permanently put in a posture of paying for themselves *and* generating an annual surplus that could be used by the entire university. The idea became "an earned income policy." The institutional problem then became how to implement the policy to generate significant income. If the government were to go on making cuts, or hold back on future funding increases, that additional income would have to be major. The policy pointed strongly toward entrepreneurial action. The gathering of funds would have to be done yearly; it would have to be systematized and administered; it would undoubtedly require some risky funding of new units; and it would require many, if not all, departments to behave in new ways. In short, it would require the elements highlighted in our analysis, developing over time in interaction with one another.

The *idea* of earned income was given organizational footing as it developed hand in hand with the creation and growth of a number of units at Warwick that were to compose an enlarged *developmental periphery*. Foremost in its unusual nature as well as its contribution to earned income has been the Warwick Manufacturing Group (WMG), set up in 1980 and directed ever since by a charismatic professor, Kumar Bhattacharyya, in the university's engineering department, a group committed fully to research *and* development (R&D) in close collaboration with major industrial firms. Bhattacharyya started out in industry and drew his staff largely from the outside world. He saw the group's mission as working "with companies, predominantly in the engineering sector, to develop the people and technology for the change process." Not only would the group work directly on changes in products and manufacturing operations but it would also work to change the "change-managers" who must "understand the technology as well as the business environment" – that is, essentially product-oriented research and engineering-based management training, in contradistinction to business school training heavy on "management" but light on understanding "product" and production processes. (University of Warwick, 1994b) Enormously creative, if not an engineering genius, Bhattacharyya developed in the 1980s a track record of inventiveness and production problem solving that caused major firms to beat a path to his door to obtain tailor-made R&D and access to the group's training programs. Over 300 firms came to be linked to the group, including such weighty ones as Rolls Royce and Rover in auto design and British Aerospace in aircraft production: "Rather than a paper exercise in partnership, WMG amounts to a members-only R&D club." (*The Economist*, Nov. 11, 1995, p. 72)

Ever ambitious to promote "international best practice," especially for British industry, and with firms lined up to join the group, expansion became phenomenal. Overseas locations for the group's work – "satellite operations" – were developed in Hong Kong, Bangkok, Kuala Lumpur, Calcutta, Nanjing, and Johannesburg; together with local staff, training courses were given by Warwick-based staff on three-to-four-week visits. Many foreign students enrolled in the group's programs at Warwick, contributing to the university's income from foreign student fees. The group's work became so extensive at home that it has required a dedicated conference center in need of expansion every few years. New buildings have gone up in the form of an Advanced Technology Centre and an International Manufacturing Centre. The latter opened in 1994 and was extended in 1996. By 1995, the WMG, with a faculty-researcher staff of over 200, had over 100 doctoral students, over 1,000 masters students and over 3,000 company staff on diploma and other "postexperience" programs each year, where course work is equal to about one-half the masters requirement. (University of Warwick, 1995d)

In a 1995 full-page treatment, *The Economist* appropriately headlined Bhattacharyya as "the professor of product development." It noted his prescience in establishing a close link between university and industry long before it became fashionable, important in a country considered short on recognition for engineering and inclined to do manufacturing the old-fashioned way. Particularly taken as eye-opening news in the mid-1990s was the claim "that Europe's biggest postgraduate center for engineering research and development should be at a British university. . . " (*The Economist*, Nov. 11, 1995, p. 72) Biggest or not, the manufacturing group represents enormous outreach. Incorporating business firms as partners in its midst, the group operates so much as a boundary-spanning unit that we can see it in part as an independent body located halfway between university and outside industry, linking the two. But since it is formally located within the university's traditional engineering department, we can also see it as a part of the *academic heartland* that has reached to the outside in a vigorous entrepreneurial fashion. In this striking case, periphery and heartland are interactive, closely fused elements.

The business school at Warwick similarly reaches out and fuses developmental programs with heartland structures. Established in 1967, just two years after the campus opened, the school has grown greatly around a wide range of MBA and executive-training programs offered in Britain – full-time and part-time, on and off campus – and abroad. Outreach growth in the mid-1990s had led to almost 2,000 managers "currently studying for the Warwick MBA, either one year full-time or over several years on a part-time basis, through evening, distance learning or modular study." (University of Warwick, 1995b, p. 96) The research interests of the school also have great outreach: beyond five "teaching groups," the school is structured in eight or more research units that reach out, for example, to the promotion of small and medium-size firms, the reform of health services, and the improvement of local government. (University of Warwick, 1993b) With such renowned scholars of the business world and organizational behavior as Andrew Pettigrew and David Storey on board, the school's academic standing was high, with top ratings in the country's research assessments and a reputation as one of the best UK business schools. By the mid-1990s, it had grown to over 130 academic teaching and research staff and over 3,000 "full-time, part-time and distance learning students pursuing a wide range of postgraduate, undergraduate and post-experience programmes." (University of Warwick, 1994a) It awarded over 400 MBA degrees a year; doctoral students numbered 160, drawn from over 25 countries. The school finances much of its work: its foreign students studying at Warwick added substantially to the university's earned income from student fees.

Conference centers are a third major item in Warwick's developmental periphery. They related closely to the work of the manufacturing group and the business school, to the point where all three of the university's major centers are known also as "management training centers." WMG has full use of an ever-expanding Arden House; the business school carries out its local outreach largely in Arden House and Scarman House. Hosting conferences and visitors for all departments, and offering desirable office and training facilities for a few outside firms, the houses win national awards year after year as premier conference centers. Top of the line services are offered and prices are set to cover costs plus a contribution to the general pot of earned income. The national Committee of University Vice-Chancellors and Principals (CVCP) has met at Scarman, reportedly with its distinguished members duly impressed and envious. Even American universities, normally fast off the mark in such matters, may here find some instructive lessons: nowhere in the huge network of several hundred American universities, large and small, do we find a general conference complex of similar scope and quality.

With the manufacturing group and the business school leading the way, foreign students, defined as non-European Union as well as non-UK citizens, together constitute a major outreach component. Along with those who are regularly enrolled full-time students, many are taught in centers abroad and others come to the main campus for short-term course work. They total up as a major source of university earned income; they spread the name of the university far and wide, especially in the fast-developing societies of Asia. "Internationalization," a favorite cliché among universities, is here given very concrete meaning.

And then there is the major Warwick Science Park, a successful undertaking begun in 1984 (in the second wave of UK science parks, after Cambridge and Heriot-Watt). It embodies entrepreneurship in its own leadership and operational style. A combined effort of university, city, and county, physically located adjacent to the campus, the park operates independently under its own board. Barclays Bank helped immensely to set it on a successful path by taking an equity position in the anchor incubator unit or venture center in place of a loan with interest. Barclays wanted a relationship to the university that would link the bank to high technology companies and their activities. The park, focused on high-tech firms, has steadily expanded around both start-up firms nourished by advice and space and the research arms of firms that want a presence in the park and at Warwick. By the mid-1990s, some 65 firms, with 1,300 employees, were situated on a 42 acre site. Major firms, such as Computervision and Sun Microsystems, are tenants. A large number of the companies located in the park have a working relationship with the manufacturing group, either in product development or staff training or both. (University of Warwick, 1995e)

In 1995 the park's director, David Rowe, and board were busy looking for new opportunities and linkages. They stressed that a reexamination of strategy was warranted after a decade of development to take the park successfully into the twenty-first century. Items on the agenda included satellite parks in the nearby region, greater systematic linkage of potential investors with small, new technology firms, an expanded program to involve undergraduates in science-based firms, and collaboration projects, funded by the European Union, with institutions in France, Belgium, and Germany. The park had caught national attention: the London *Times*, in a major two-page article in late 1994, proclaimed "its remarkable success" as "Warwick's bold experiment to create a hothouse environment for the nurture of high technology companies." The park had an "image and reputation" that encourage firms to join its "balanced population of companies." (London *Times*, 1994, pp. 22–23)

The science park, together with the manufacturing group, the business school, and several other university units – for example, an Industrial Development Office – not reviewed here, have given Warwick a complex, well developed university-industry interface. A 1993 study by a German consulting firm for a French regional development agency compared the interface developed in six "best practice" institutions in six European nations. Based on recommendations from industrial managers, the institutions examined included such notables as the famous Federal Institute of Technology (ETH) in Switzerland, the Karlsruhe Technical University in Germany, and the Technical University of Compiègne in France. Warwick was the only research/comprehensive university nominated by industrialists for this study; all the others were known as technical universities. Warwick "came out first," judged "able to initiate and maintain business relationships more effectively than any other analyzed university," and thus served as "the outstanding example of how a university should interact with industry to accomplish the needs of both sides." The study took note of the influence of university govern-ance structures, pointing out that at Warwick – apropos of our element of strengthened steering core – that a "centralized strategy" involved central management in all major decisions. (University of Warwick, 1993a) The periphery at the university clearly contains an interface with industry that is world-class.

But the periphery is not limited to this interface. Facing outward on a large scale is an arts complex located at the heart of the campus, with a set of theatres, halls, and galleries for events in the performing arts (drama, music, dance, film, visual arts) that draw over 250,000 attendances a year. A well-developed Department of Continuing Education offers a wide range of courses for adults, a unit operating on and off campus that in the mid-1990s involved over 8,000 registered students and also carried out extensive research in its specialty. The university has aggressively pursued the establishment of outside services on campus, e.g., banks, barbershop, bookstore and news agency. All such services are self-supporting and appear on the ledgers of earned income. Warwick may be "green-fields" in its origin, but it has worked hard to make itself a part of "the community" as well as a university close to industry.

All the above outreach activities were assisted and advanced in their development by a *strengthened administrative core* that arguably is the most important of all the pathways taken to transform Warwick. In the balance between central control and departmental autonomy, this core is relatively centralized. As we shall see in later chapters, the other four institutions analyzed in this study – Twente, Strathclyde, Chalmers, and Joensuu – emphasized the decentralization of funds and administration to faculties or departments that constitute basic unit levels. The idea of decentralization has been a theme in reform in Europe during the late 1980s and 1990s, following the twin desires to break up State-led rigidities and to make more space at local levels for the leading role that specialized experts need to play in making judgments within increasingly complex bundles of knowledge. But Warwick has set its face against this theme, arguing instead that, yes, strong departments are needed – we have them and will nurture them – but we particularly want a strong center that will stand for the overall institutional interest and offer an effective guiding hand.

As part of this posture, the university has not created faculties as a strong form of organization between center and department: in 1995 despite increasing pressure from growth in size and complexity, faculty deans were notable for their absence. The institution prides itself on a "flat structure" of center and department. Departments have remained the building blocks of the university and their chairs have a significant role. The chairs relate directly to the vice-chancellor and such senior administrative offices as the registrar and finance officer. They also do not relate to a single apex committee, a structure we observe later in other settings, but to a set of interrelated central committees, knitted together by overlapping membership, consisting of a small cadre of senior administrators together with a small group of professors elected by colleagues to play central roles. This web of interlocked central committees has become the heart of Warwick's capacity to steer itself.

During the first 15 years of the institution's life, the years before 1980, Vice-Chancellor Jack Butterworth, for reasons of personality and position as founding "V-C," often operated with a strong hand. But as we saw at the outset, he did not set up an overall blueprint, but instead set himself the task of finding excellent scholars and turning them loose to build various departments. Departmentalism soon had strong roots, while the center remained unelaborated. In retrospect, the critical step toward a different kind of central core was the strong response to the Thatcher challenge Butterworth and Michael Shattock, the registrar, devised. They turned the earned income idea into the Earned Income Policy; the policy was soon put in the hands of an Earned Income Group formally established in 1984–1985. Strongly led by the registrar, the group became the gathering point for discretionary monies. It became *the* instrument for entrepreneurial action on adding revenue, the central place for the year-by-year hard work of finding and mining new veins of income.

After developing new sources throughout the 1980s, the group in the 1990s has garnered over 50 units on campus that pay their way and which, in nearly all cases, are expected to come up with a surplus. The group "top-slices" various incomes generated by the manufacturing group, the business school, and the conference centers. It expects a "profit" from the bookstore and the barbershop. Professional managers are hired to run the various units in a businesslike up-scale fashion, and can be fired, as in private business, when they do not do the job. An able deputy finance officer closely monitors the group's portfolio, on a 90-day basis.

To observe meetings of the Earned Income Group is to see a collegial form of crispness in university administration. The registrar, deputy registrar, academic registrar, finance officer, deputy finance officer, university treasurer (a lay member of court) are all there, joined by several senior faculty members who serve as pro vice-chancellors elected for two-year terms with a limit of six years. Accounts are closely studied for current performance against set targets. Various managers in charge of different operations may be called in; successful performances are praised, operations running "below the line" are queried on what has gone wrong and what remedial action is needed. Several accounts – an example is the one devoted to income from student residencies – are expected only to break even. But all the others must operate under the dictate of earning income.

The earned money, together with income from the more standardized governmental annual allocations, passes over to committees focused on overall budget review and internal allocation. As in other UK universities the committees largely exist as spin-offs from Council and Senate, the two overarching bodies. Senior administrative officers are "in attendance" at meetings of all the important decision-making committees, those expected "to push the business forward." A key role is played by the Joint Council and Senate Strategy Committee, created in the mid-1980s that brings together financial, academic, and physical plant planning in one place, a place for macrostrategy. Membership includes the council's chairman, treasurer, and building (sub)committee chair, all highly experienced business executives long committed to Warwick. Notably, the university has not had any "capital money" – money for construction of buildings – from the national government since 1984, forcing it "to pick it up" by going to a "private financing mode." Thus the linkage of recurrent and capital money has come together more tightly within the university, and then is linked to "academic things" in the remit of the Joint Strategy Committee. The committee became in 1988 the center of rolling-forward five-year planning ("finance-driven" rather than "academic-driven") in which decisions about how much money can be made available are made first, followed by hard decisions on what to develop and what to let go on the academic side.

A second key role at the center is played by a senate committee that allocates sums to departments and controls faculty positions. Vacated posts revert to the committee for reassignment or discontinuance. Heads of departments have to make their case for personnel directly to this "hands-on" central group that functions as a microacademic strategy body. The committee is chaired by a faculty member elected as a pro vice-chancellor. Three faculty serve as elected members from the three main subject areas of sciences, social sciences, and humanities. Three other faculty also come from these broad sectors as elected heads of area boards. In lieu of deans, professors who chair the faculty boards come to serve on this and other key central committees. The system depends on a gradually rotating cadre of professors who are willing to serve in such heavy-duty central assignments and thereby bring traditional faculty points of view into central circles that otherwise might be dominated by what faculty would view as the managerial outlook of administrative officers. By much informal as well as formal contact, the committees link faculty with administration.

Without extensive decentralization to faculty and departmental levels, Warwick has effected collegial steerage by means of these central committees in which senior officers, some lay members of the council, and faculty members share responsibilities. With faculty clearly involved, hard choices can be made in supporting new initiatives and realigning traditional allocations of resources. The core incorporates the academic heartland into the center. In this structure, a university can be entrepreneurial without the CEO (the chief executive officer), the vice-chancellor in this case, necessarily being entrepreneurial. Warwick's second "V-C," Clark Brundin (1985–1992), was not: in effect, the committee system had taken on the role. The third and current V-C, Sir Brian Follett (1993-) believes he was selected not because he was an entrepreneur, nor did he seek the position to become one. With a strong academic background in chemistry and biology, and experience in national science councils and funding bodies, his personal mission emphasized the strengthening of the sciences at Warwick. In short, steering capacity has been institutionalized in a committee structure that blends lay council members, elected academic representatives, and senior administrative officers.

The strength of Warwick's collegial central steerage was exhibited in the mid-1990s in the complete restructuring of the education faculty, which was made part of the university with the merger of an adjacent college of education in the late 1970s. A Faculty of Education with five internal departments had become a special problem, particularly because of up and down government action on the supply side of teacher education. In this area of activity, the government had become notoriously undependable and the faculty had gradually undergone much downsizing. In 1995 the university closed the departments and abolished the faculty, and was able to say with justice it was all done with the consent of the involved academics: they voted to abolish and to take up a new residence as an institute of education within the Faculty of Social Studies. Early retirements helped out. The university was then also able to say, as proof of capacity to realign traditional structure, that it had moved from a four-faculty university to a three-faculty one. The reorganization could also be considered as "up-market."

As chartered and administered through the system of central committees, the earned-income approach at Warwick is muscled by a strong capacity to "top-slice and cross-subsidize." This capacity is the backbone of the ability to come to the aid of departments (and specialties within them) that cannot readily raise money on their own, and to back completely new ventures. As the registrar explained to European rectors in a 1994 conference (Shattock, 1994a, p. 4):

> Some departments, e.g., the Business School and Engineering, are more obviously capable of generating external income than say Sociology or the History of Art but because, once the departmental share is separated off, the university's share [the top slice] is simply pooled with government funds and allocated on academic criteria, all departments benefit. It is accepted that it is to the university's advantage that those departments that can generate income should support those departments that are simply unable to do so [the cross-subsidy].

Departments that regularly have monies taken away in this fashion are, of course, not always happy about it. The center then has to have the power and legitimacy to say "it is accepted" because this is the way we build the university as a whole.

The Warwick structure tests the limits of centralized decision making in a university that steadily grows larger and more complex. An in-house study of the "research challenges facing Warwick," carried out by Andrew Pettigrew and Ewan Ferlie in late 1995, probed faculty attitudes on centralization versus decentralization and the locus of decision making for new initiatives. (Pettigrew and Ferlie, 1996) Some faculty were critical of the existing system: "there is now the danger of Warwick becoming middle-aged and over-bureaucratized"; "the financial management system at Warwick is archaic. It's massively centralised. I would like to see large scale operational devolution to departments plus a greater strategic thrust from the Centre"; "greater decentralization is needed. The Centre can't get involved with all the 1000 flowers – only the major ones that eventually matter"; "there are no clear decision making lines in the university. So one is shifted from committee to committee and eventually decisions are made out of committee in your absence"; "there is a lack of crispness of responsibility." (pp. 24–26)

But others were still much impressed: "Warwick is a very good place to work because you can get on with doing the job"; "The university has been absolutely brilliant. . . We have had glitches but I cannot fault the university. In fact this is what has kept me going"; "The whole point of coming to Warwick was that the access to the Centre was there. It was very short, there were no trails of bureaucracy and hierarchy and faculties and schools and heads of this and that. . . . That to me immediately was the green light"; "Compared with other universities this one can make positive commitments to a new and innovative area" (p. 15).

The senior administrators and faculty most committed to Warwick's evolved steering core could still, as of the mid-1990s, take pride in its apparent role in the institution's success. They could stress that the governance and decision-making structure was surely not broken and hence did not need radical fixing. The structure had acquired a legitimized momentum difficult to disrupt. But growing size and operational complexity have increasingly threatened to overload it, especially with such large units as the business school and the engineering department. This leaves open the possibility down the road of greater decentralization to school or department level, coupled with selective, strategic steering from the center.

All that we have reviewed thus far about the power of the institutional idea of "earning our way," the extensive organizational periphery, and the power-fully centralized steering core relate to a fourth element, a richly *diversified funding base*. Warwick is at the cutting edge of a general trend in the financing of European universities: less governmental support as a share of the whole, more support from nongovernmental (particularly noneducation ministry) sources. To simplify: income streams for individual public universities take three main forms. Stream 1, mainline state allocation, is a standardized mode of traditional finance, with funds commonly based on some combination of numbers of students, faculty, and even physical plant space. Stream 2, funds obtained from governmental research councils, is a mode that differentiates among universities according to the degree their professors, departments, and research groups win and lose competitions for research grants and contracts; and Stream 3, income from all other sources, differentiates universities extensively as funds are or are not obtained from industry, philanthropic foundations, local, regional, and national government departments other than the main education-ministry source, and from the European Union, student fees, endowment income, and surpluses or profits earned on a variety of campus self-supporting operations. The worldwide trend, reflected in Europe in the cases that follow from The Netherlands, Scotland, Sweden, and Finland, shows income shifting from nearly total dependence on the first stream to greater reliance on an array of sources, particularly those here lumped together as a third stream. And the trend is accelerated by entrepreneurship. Entrepreneurial universities seek third-stream sources and actively reach out to them.

Warwick's earned-income policy has done precisely that. Early on it pushed hard to raise monies that were not allocated by government. Its income figures for 1995 showed that in a total budget of approximately 134 million pounds, just 51 million (38 percent) came from the Higher Education Funding Council (England), together with grants for teacher training from a national Teacher Training Agency. Income from research grants and contracts came to about 15 percent, 9 percent from governmental research councils and 6 percent from nongovernmental sources. All other support, nearly 50 percent and increasing, came from additional third-stream sources. These included fees from overseas students (who pay full cost) and vocational/short courses, approximately 16 million (12 percent); and other income from sources noted in our discussion of the developmental periphery, totaling over 37 million pounds (30 percent), including management training centers, catering and conferences, and campus retail operations. The trend from 1970 on that led to these mid-1990 income shares is shown in Table 2–1: mainline government support dropped from about 70 to less than 40 percent during the 1980–1995 years; third-stream sources increased as a share of the whole from about 20 to nearly 50 percent; second and third streams together had become about two-thirds of all income.

TABLE 2:1.
Sources of Financial Support, Warwick University, 1970–1995 (millions of pounds)

	Core Support		Research Grants and Contracts*		All Other Sources		Total	
Year	Amount	Percent	Amount	Percent	Amount	Percent	Amount	Percent
1970	2.0	69	0.3	10	0.6	21	2.9	100
1975	5.1	69	0.7	9	1.6	22	7.4	100
1980	14.6	70	2.0	10	4.3	20	20.9	100
1985	21.5	60	4.8	13	9.8	27	36.1	100
1990	36.0	43	14.6	18	31.9	39	82.5	100
1995	51.3	38	19.7	15	63.0	47	134.0	100

*Includes research grants and contracts from both governmental and nongovernmental sources; e.g., in 1995, the governmental source was about nine percent, the nongovernmental totaled about six percent, making a total of fifteen percent.
Source: trend data gathered by Paul Anderson, Assistant Registrar, Warwick University

The Earned Income Policy began as a way to fill the gap left by the state when it started systematic reduction in support in the early 1980s. Earned Income has done that and more. It has provided the means for new initiatives. It has provided the funds for cross-subsidy to academic departments and subjects that bring in little or no extra money but are viewed as institutionally worthy of continuing support and enhancement.

But more income is always needed: universities are expensive and good universities are very expensive. In the mid-1990s, Warwick decided to adopt the step it had shunned in the early 1980s when it voiced the doctrine that we will go out and earn money rather than beg for it. Oxford and Cambridge, with their towering prestige and unmatched well-to-do alumni, had just shown that major sums could be secured through organized "fundraising." Warwick decided in 1995 to commit to a long-term effort along this line: it now had an estimable reputation and loyal alumni. The effort would entail short-term pain for many campus units: to hire a first-class Director of Public Affairs and a Development Officer and provide them with resources to tackle the job in a major way, 500,000 pounds had to be "clawed back" from the existing budget. Once the Joint Strategy Committee made the decision to go this route – to seek major long-term enhancement of discretionary income from some combination of annual gift-giving and endowment income – and do it now rather than at some undefined later date, the senior administrative officers had to take some funds from one academic unit after another. They were, in effect, required to cross-subsidize a development venture from academic programs and early retirements. The capacity to do so was another example of the power of the center to assert the institutional interest by mounting a new initiative and finding the means, from a tight budget, to effect it. Serious payback here, if the new fundraising infrastructure is successful, may be eight to ten years down the road.

This brings us to the fifth pivotal element, *the stimulated academic heartland*. Entrepreneurship has not been left to a few subject areas such as engineering and business, and only to a managerial group dedicated to earning income, but has come to characterize virtually all academic fields. Four features reveal much about the involvement of core academic units: the melding of periphery into the core; the extensive building of research centers under departments; the construction of a universitywide graduate school; and the introduction of an imaginative and highly attractive research fellowship scheme that reached across the campus.

Periphery-heartland fusion has developed in the two largest programs we noted in our discussion of the developmental periphery. The huge Warwick Manufacturing Group clearly exists as a quasi-independent entity; it even goes "off-scale" in much of its salary-and-career structure in order to attract unusual talent in competition with the lures of industry. On the university-industry interface, the group lies close to industry. But it is also very much a formal part of Warwick's omnibus single engineering department and appears as such in its campus location. One can find it by entering the engineering department as well as by tracking its independent ways. The business school is even more a fusion of outreach to heartland. It bulks large in the forming of a productive periphery, with quasi-independent programs multiplying around the Masters in Business Administration (MBA) degrees, each a veritable "tub-on-its-own bottom." But it remains foremost a major academic unit, with all programs subsumed under its administration and general campus review. The only major unit in the periphery that stands fully independent is the science park, operating under its own board and off the books of the university's administration.

All others are simultaneously a part of the academic heartland. And even the park has quasi-formal and informal links to the academic departments, particularly to engineering.

Departments at Warwick, virtually without exception, have been busy developing research centers to further their own subjects, necessitating the raising of funds from second- and third-income streams. Such efforts have not simply been left to "science and technology," where large amounts are most likely to be available. The university's 1995 annual report depicted current structure in three major groupings: Social Studies, Arts, and Science. The social science component consisted of nine departments and schools and over 20 research centers. The units responsible for teaching ranged from economics, sociology, and politics to continuing education and applied social studies; they included a school of law and the very large business school. The numerous research centers operating largely under the departments and schools included ones on legal research, health services, philosophy and literature, as well as on macroeconomic modeling, comparative labor studies, ethnic relations, democratization, women and gender.

The arts component showed nine departments and schools and six research centers. The departments consisted of history, history of art, classics and ancient history, English and comparative literature, French, German, Italian, theatre studies, and film and television; the research centers included one in general humanities research as well as more targeted ones in cultural studies, social history, and the Renaissance. The entrepreneurial spirit shows through in these departments and centers. For example: the head of theatre studies, Professor David Thomas, reported in interview that he was a "happy opportunist" who came to Warwick because it "had an entrepreneurial feel about it." He takes experimental performances – undergraduates may be included – out to international festivals and audiences, raising money as he goes, while training "cultural administrators" in advanced programs in a "research-led department." With self-funding courses, the department is basically self-supporting: it "washes its own face."

The science component was constituted by nine departments and schools and five research centers. The teaching units consisted of engineering and a new School of Postgraduate Medical Education as well as such traditional science fields as physics, chemistry, and biology. The research centers included the large Centre for Advanced Materials Technology which has joint research projects with such major British industrial partners as Rolls Royce and British Gas, as well as foreign collaborative ventures in such countries as Sweden, France, Belgium, and Japan.

Across the three faculties in 1995, Warwick consisted of 27 major departments and schools (with some subdepartments) and, as a second major operating component, over 30 research centers. The university has dampened department proliferation: for example, English and comparative literature are together in one department in the humanities, all the biological sciences are grouped in one biology department, and anthropology is left out altogether in the social sciences. Departments are thereby made relatively large, achieving critical mass in the included subjects. Fewer than 30 basic departments provide some focus: the university explicitly makes the point that it does not attempt to achieve the coverage of subjects found in the 100 and more departments of the large UK civic universities. The bias is toward focused comprehensiveness.

The growing use of research centers and the resulting dual operating structure of departments and centers strongly indicates diffusion of the entrepreneurial attitude throughout the academic understructure. At the cutting edge of this spread we find in 1995 the Warwick business school raising over three-quarters of its budget from "earned-income activities in teaching, consulting, and research, while just under a quarter came from Higher Education Funding Council grants." (University of Warwick, 1995b, p. 97) Other departments are not far behind. The university proudly points to the dominant role of the academic heartland units in producing income; it is able to claim that over two-thirds of its earned income (70 percent in 1995) is academically driven, that is, "based in academic departments and concerned with the provision of teaching and research on a fee-paying basis." (University of Warwick, 1995a, p. 9)

Further, Warwick has developed two major initiatives in the 1990s that range across its stimulated heartland. The first was the establishment in 1991 of a universitywide graduate school, the first of its kind in the United Kingdom. Like most European systems of universities, the British system has long lacked a formally organized structure for supporting systematic instruction for graduate students (known as postgraduate in Britain), especially for research students pursuing the doctorate. (Becher, 1993; Clark, 1995) British universities made a delayed and essentially secondary commitment to the graduate level. The modern Ph.D. was not put in place until 1918, virtually half a century after its introduction and takeoff in the 1870s and 1880s in the United States. Adopted in the form of a three-year program, the doctorate was almost completely given over to actual engagement in research, a practice that has continued to dominate. A British expert on the training of researchers writing in the early 1980s noted: "At present we assume that the need for researchers is best met by selecting some of our academically most able graduates and giving them three years in which to carry out one major research project and write a thesis." (Hirsh, 1982, p.190) Future researchers were deemed not to need more instruction in courses. There would be nothing like the American graduate school with its overarching panoply of rules and regulations for admissions, course credits, written and oral examinations, and dissertations.

But postgraduate work grew in the late 1980s and the 1990s in an ad hoc fashion, field by field, especially in what the British called "taught masters" programs. Doctoral students became more numerous nationwide and in specific universities; they placed a heavy burden on the happenstance of individualized mentor-apprentice relationships while offering up more clusters of advanced students that could become the critical mass for organized courses. Graduate student complaints about uneven, if not poor, supervision increased (Becher, 1993) amid general observations that graduate education was "bolted on" to the structure for undergraduate education on the one side and on to staff research on the other, marginalizing it with poor systematic support.

Warwick, reflecting its proactive, searching style, was apparently the first university in Europe to seek to systematically remedy the problem by establishing a full graduate school, American-style, that would embrace all masters and doctoral programs. An initial paper prepared by Michael Shattock, the registrar, led to an exploratory working group in 1989. A young administrator, John Hogan, was sent to the United States to observe the working of the graduate school at the University of Wisconsin and to attend meetings of the U.S. Council of Graduate Schools: his follow-on report influenced the way Warwick developed its new school. Robert Burgess, a professor of sociology, was on the early team and became the first chair of the new unit and its board when they got underway in 1991. Warwick was strongly interested in adding graduate students, as reported earlier, and as part of the rapid expansion of the late 1980s and early 1990s the university found that its number of graduate students had more than doubled in five years. This led to over 4,600 full and part-time, or nearly 40 percent of the total student population, a very high proportion for a publicly supported comprehensive university. (University of Warwick, 1992–93, p. 2) Additional curricular, financial, and social support for this now large population could have been developed by individual departments (or faculties) in an ad hoc fashion – this did occur later at Twente, Chalmers, and Joensuu on the continent – but Warwick opted for the American all-inclusive form that then evolved in Britain as "the Warwick model." (Burgess, 1996)

Across the university, the new school was given the remit to regulate the admission and monitor the progress of graduate students, to provide appropriate academic resources and social facilities for them, to make awards to them from set-aside university funds, and, overall, "to scrutinize all new postgraduate degrees and course proposals" and "to review all graduate programmes on a three-year cycle." (Burgess, 1996, p. 12) In short order the school developed a teaching assistants' scheme, designating a training program and employment for up to four years, and research assistantships of similar lengths. New residences were constructed, and a postgraduate association initiated by the students themselves. As the locus for systematic, periodic review of all postgraduate degrees and for the monitoring of student progress in pursuit of advanced degrees, the new school was soon the place that could say, in American style, that *it* "now offers over 130 postgraduate programmes." (University of Warwick, 1992–1993, p. 5) Applicants and enrolled students continued to increase: the latter from 4,600 in 1992–1993 to 5,200 two years later (University of Warwick, 1995c, p. 7)

In retrospect, the establishment of a formal universitywide graduate school in 1991 was clearly the right move at the right time. Other universities were showing interest: establishing a stronger infrastructure for advanced degree work was about to become the thing to do. *The Times Higher Education Supplement* (*THES*) noted in early 1994 that Warwick had "definitely stolen a march on everyone else," that "institutions with a graduate school, most notably Warwick University, which established one in 1991, are seen to have a distinct publicity advantage over rivals." (April 15, 1994, p. 1) Not only was Warwick fast off the mark and thorough in its effort, but it immediately moved to promote graduate schools nationally. Burgess convened a meeting on the topic at the university in January 1993 for interested parties at other universities and nearly 100 people came. That summer, six months later, a more formal first conference at Warwick was convened, with Jules LaPidus, longtime head of the American Council of Graduate Schools, as featured speaker. Chaired by Burgess, in early 1994 a UK Council for Graduate Education was established; it was soon able to claim more than 90 institutional members. No government approval was needed and none was sought. By the end of 1994, about 20 universities had formally established graduate schools. Universities were finding out at a rapid rate that "the postgraduate market [offered] a way of maintaining the momentum built up over the past few years of increasing student numbers." (*THES*, Aug. 5, 1994, p. 7) While the government had "slammed on the brakes" on full-time undergraduate education, because of its costs, officials cast an approving eye on low-cost "taught masters" programs, with students paying much of the bill. And since universities wanted to build doctoral programs, and national research council funds for doctoral support were meager, the institutions were willing to invest more of their own funds (if available!) for teaching and research assistantships.

Warwick's leadership in promoting new infrastructures for graduate education also spread to the continent. In 1994 Burgess coauthored a book with an Austrian colleague which reviewed graduate education reform in six European countries, with attention paid to the development of systematic training components. (Burgess and Schratz, 1994) Collaborative research was started in 1995 in six European countries that stretched geographically from the UK to Greece. A widespread diffusion effect was underway.

In 1994–1995, Warwick offered up yet another striking initiative that revealed much about its ability to see what ought to be done, mount the will to devise a programmatic solution, and then move relatively fast administratively to put it in place. The initiative was the Warwick Research Fellowships, started by a paper drawn up at the vice-chancellor's request in late spring, 1994 to discuss "how Warwick might increase the number of high quality research active staff through a research fellowship scheme." The idea was pursued on a fast track: detailed proposals were approved by the university's senate in July, a few months later; departments and research centers were immediately informed and invited to bid for fellows. The basic units had to decide on internal priorities that could be advanced by fellows focused in certain areas and to exhibit a capacity to fund one-third of each post acquired and filled. Departmental replies were evaluated in a central fellowship Committee, an overall institutional listing was assembled of preferred fields, and worldwide advertising, including on the Internet, was begun in the early fall, with mid-November deadlines set for applications. (University of Warwick, 1996)

Administrative (and departmental) staff work then became enormous: the 50 advertised posts received about 8,500 inquiries, and a follow-on 2,000 applications. Applications went to the departments for rankings and then back to the central committee in December and January. One hundred and forty applicants scattered across many countries were shortlisted for interview, invited to the university, and seen by interview panels in February. Decisions were made in March to make offers to 49 candidates, of whom 36 later accepted – seventeen in the sciences, eleven in the humanities, and eight in the social sciences. Of those who accepted, 44 percent were from overseas (19 percent from European Union countries, 25 percent non-EU); and 33 percent were women. The science intake was particularly international, with 71 percent from overseas. The university held the number to the 36 who accepted, rather than fill in with a second round to get to the upper-end target of 50. The appointed fellows then came on board at the beginning of the 1995–1996 academic year. (University of Warwick, 1996)

The whole exercise may be seen as proof positive that universities can move very fast across the board when they have the will and a sharpened administrative capacity to do so. In his initial memorandum to chairs of departments in the summer of 1994, Vice-Chancellor Sir Brian Follett stressed "the great importance that the university is placing on the scheme. It is a key step towards further enhancing and strengthening Warwick's standing in research. To be successful, we will have to appoint research fellows of the highest quality, comparable with those awarded long-term personal fellowships by the Royal Society, the British Academy, the Research Councils, etc. This will not be easy, but the scheme will fail unless it is achieved." (University of Warwick, 1996) The will expressed by the V-C was soon picked up and rapidly advanced in the central committees and the departments. And a highly focused bit of administrative machinery was created and placed in the hands of a bright, capable young assistant registrar who then managed on a tight schedule the enormous flow of communication within the university and between the university and outside interested parties, applicants, and awardees.

The successful applicants were offered attractive positions: six-year appointments as research scholars, located in departments where teaching was not to exceed one-third a normal load, and with a strong promise that if they were productive – that is, "establish themselves as international leaders in their areas of research" – they would at the end of this initial appointment become permanent members of the faculty. Those selected already had a publication record that augured well for the future. The university's immediate hope was that the young fellows would "galvanize research generally, act as research foci, increase research grant income and postgraduate numbers." The long-term hope was to renew the faculty by replacing retiring professors and improving the age profile of the faculty, especially to heighten the number of young staff in the sciences. The age of the new fellows ranged from 27 to 37, the average being 32. This was close to "the target age range of 'late twenties/early thirties'." (University of Warwick, 1996) By the end of the fellows' first year, the university had good reason to think that the whole exercise, especially at a dreary time when nationally awarded research fellowships were in notoriously short supply, amounted to a first-class and probably successful initiative.

The gain in reputation, at least, was immediate and clear. In September 1994 the *THES* editorialized about how universities were being short-changed by a government that persisted over many years in driving down unit costs, causing the universities to pursue money primarily to support an underfunded system and "too little by genuine educational considerations." Warwick was then portrayed as the leading example to the contrary (*THES*, Sept. 30, 1994, p. 11):

> Warwick University's announcement this week that it has made sufficient profits from non-government funded activities to be able to take on 50 research fellows on six-year contracts is a heartening example. This is an investment in academic quality which would once have been made from the public purse but the public purse no longer funds excellence adequately. It is a supreme irony that Warwick, once vilified for commercial attitudes which were thought to compromise academic integrity, is now unusual in having money to spend on academic enrichment. Alas, not all universities are as well placed.

A few weeks later *The Economist* (Nov. 12, 1994, p. 74) sharply commended the university, on the eve of its thirtieth birthday, for its "enthusiasm for the private sector" that had "paid off handsomely." Noting that the national funding council had rated the university as "Britain's fifth-best research university and also given it high marks as a teaching institution," *The Economist* maintained that:

> Warwick looks set to grow even stronger. While other British universities struggle to make ends meet, Warwick is splashing out £10m ($16m) on hiring 50 research fellows in a range of academic disciplines. . . Few other British universities could even contemplate dispensing such largess. . . Warwick can afford the research fellowships because, since the early 1980s, it has committed itself to generating private income. . . Some of Warwick's competitors are copying its example rather than carping. Cambridge, which has traditionally depended on appeals and endowments for its funding, has struck "corporate partnerships" with companies such as Glaxo; the London School of Economics has set up a private company to sell its research.

Two months later, the *THES* (January 27, 1995, p. 6) chimed in again with a highly favorable portrayal that any university public relations officer would kill for. In an article entitled "Warwick joins fellowship elite," the new research fellowships (WRFs) were seen as a scheme which is set to challenge the Oxbridge dominance of the postdoctoral market. . . They run for six years – double the time of the typical Oxbridge JRF [junior research fellowship] – and more strikingly, they offer the prospect of a permanent post for those scholars who establish an international reputation. . . Brian Follett, Warwick's vice-chancellor, says that the WRFs are pitched higher than the JRFs, and are comparable with the Royal Society university research fellowships. . . The 50 WRFs will transform the age profile of Warwick's lecturers. . . [The scheme] will also ensure that Warwick. . . looks good when the next research assessment comes around in 1996. . . [And, quoting the Vice-Chancellor,] Warwick has decided to recruit young researchers rather than "hoover up stars" because of a conviction that "youth is an important factor in the energy behind novel discoveries."

Four months later, the *THES* (May 5, 1995, p. 7) came back to point out that "Warwick leads as others follow" : "Universities are rushing to copy Warwick University's prestigious £10 million research fellowship scheme, launched last year to attract 50 top scholars. Among its imitators are old universities like Leeds and Manchester, but also new ones like Coventry and De Montfort." Leeds was now offering "20 fellowships per year for three to five years," Manchester "has already appointed 15 research fellows with prospects of more this year," Coventry wanted to recruit "12 research fellows in technical areas, offering a six-year package worth £26,000 per year – twice a lecturer's basic starting wage," and noted that "its neighbour's initiative" was "a very shrewd, smart thing to do." De Montfort, wanting to invest heavily in research, was now "ready to offer at least 30 six-year research fellowships." Notably, the University of Surrey announced with full-page ads in March 1995 (*THES*, March 5, 1995) that it was "investing in excellence" with 30 Foundation Lectureships, good for three years, that would "provide outstanding scholars with an ideal opportunity to concentrate on developing their research work." Senior as well as junior appointments could be made. The whole scheme would be "funded through income from the University's Foundation Fund arising from its highly successful Research Park." In a national setting of reduced governmental support, and institutional status competition sharply on the rise, UK universities were fast learning how to find discretionary income from private sources which could be invested mainly in research.

Only a month later, the *THES* (June 23, 1995, p. 4) returned to the Warwick initiative with the news that "Oxbridge dominates Warwick fellowships," in the sense that a third of the new fellowships "have been given to rising stars of Oxford and Cambridge." Out of 36 fellows appointed in 21 disciplines, 12 "currently hold posts in Oxford and Cambridge" and "16 have either studied or taught at Oxbridge." Further, the fellowships "have also been given to candidates from prestigious foreign institutions, including Berkeley, Virginia, Melbourne and L'institute Hautes Etudes Scientifique in Paris," and altogether "the international fellows come from Australia, Canada, China, Denmark, France, Germany, Holland, India, Israel, Russia, and the United States."

The data offered by the *THES* to UK academics and the general public spoke to a point that had been raised by traditionalist critics: that the whole fellowship scheme at Warwick had been nothing more than a gigantic public-relations exercise and would fail to lure the best academics away from more prestigious places, notably Oxford and Cambridge. But Warwick could and did attract them. The initiative could even be seen as a small step to help the UK reverse its braindrain, long a sore point among British academics, especially scientists, as promising young scholars fled to other countries, primarily the United States, and to UK jobs outside academia. With recruitment pursued on a thoroughly worldwide basis, the Warwick effort could even pull in talent from elsewhere that might be superior to that brought forward in the UK system: for example, out of 250 applicants in mathematics, the five mathematicians offered fellowships by Warwick were non-UK applicants. All five chose to come, giving the mathematics department, newly chaired by a mathematician from an American university, a cadre of excellent young scholars that truly reflects the highly internationalized character of this key discipline.

The Warwick fellowship scheme had a significant internal downside, however: it throws the regular junior staff into somewhat of a second-best position. Research fellows need to teach very little; they are heavily subsidized to devote themselves to research and publication. Meanwhile, the regular staff are evermore heavily involved in teaching and weighty departmental responsibilities, the price for academic influence by senate and faculty committees. "What about us?" became a natural complaint, prodding the university to pay more attention to the junior staff's conditions of work and morale, including teaching loads and time for research. Warwick staff were not prohibited from applying for the research fellowships and several, mainly in the social sciences, were selected. Overall, the fellowship scheme may be seen as putting pressure on the main career structure to move all positions in the direction of more research. Limited resources and the ever present UK concern for staff devotion to undergraduate education then become the chief constraints on the promotion of research.

Conclusion

In a decade and a half of transforming effort, Warwick made remarkable progress in achieving operational strength and high status as a comprehensive research university at the same time that it developed uncommon outreach to industry. Academic and practical thrusts interacted to promote a virtuous circle of effects. Financial and research returns from industrial outreach furthered academic goals, while an increasingly respected academic base pushed up-market in the outreach programs, especially those involving contact with industry. For academics and business executives alike, Warwick in the 1990s brought repute to those associated with it.

Proof of achievement and recognized competence has been abundant. For a university only three decades old in the mid-1990s, Warwick has had a surprisingly high number of top-rated departments in the research assessment exercises that the British government has carried out every three or four years since 1986: in the fourth such assessment in 1996, the university had 12 departments with a "5*" or "5" rating at the top of the scale, nine with the strongly favorable rating of "4," and only three at "3" and one at "2." The university could appropriately point out that it had put forward 98 percent of its faculty members for the assessment (hiding far fewer than nearly all other institutions, including Cambridge at 90 percent), and that four-fifths of its faculty were in 4- and 5-rated departments. If games had to be played with a government that was obsessed with top-down assessment, the university had positioned itself to maximize the gains in status as well as in income that flowed to those able to sustain a virtuous circle of effects at the top of the line. On one indicator after another, based on national assessment of teaching quality as well as research quality, Warwick could claim a position in the top ten British universities, often as high as fifth or sixth, placing just after Cambridge and Oxford and such impressive institutions in the national capital as the London School of Economics, University College London, and Imperial College. Potential students have gotten the message: applicants to Warwick in the mid-1990s outnumbered available places in the entering class ten to one (in 1995, 27,000 to 2,300). Apace the growing size of the applicant pool (*and* Warwick's solid standing among other preferred institutions when students make multiple applications through a central office), student selectivity has steadily risen. The institution could justly claim that it had become "one of the UK's most popular universities." (University of Warwick, 1995a)

A number of indicators placed Warwick as the most successful of the Seven Sisters, the "green-fields" universities initiated in the 1960s. It had become much the largest in overall structure, an important characteristic in a system where small size had severely constrained the competitive scale and scope needed for both student growth and knowledge growth: in 1995, over 13,000 full-time students attended, compared to Lancaster, the next largest at 8,000, and Sussex at 7,600. It had the largest income, double on the average the budgets of the other new universities and about the overall budget size (at over 130 million pounds by 1995) of some of the large civic universities that had developed in the UK's industrial cities since the late nineteenth century. The research ratings have marked it first among the Seven Sisters, with high average institutional scores stemming from the large number of "4" and "5" rated departments. An analysis made by the Vice-Chancellor of the University of Birmingham showed that in the 1989 second national research assessment Warwick had 18 high-rated departments (4s and 5s), compared to York's 11, Sussex's 10, and the remaining 4 members of the New University group with 9 or fewer. (Thompson, Sir Michael, 1991, 352–353) And Warwick's outreach to industry, a special feature, has been a qualitative leap higher. To round out its highly favorable reputation, the university could also boast that its Performing Arts Centre was the largest complex of its kind in the UK outside of London, thereby bringing "the community" physically into the university on a massive scale.

Warwick profited immensely from its early tough-minded recognition that central government in Britain had become an undependable university patron, often a hostile one. The recognition led to a will to work hard to place the institution in an independent posture – to stand on its own feet by earning its way. Building off of this willful idea, much effort, as we have seen, fed into strengthening its steering capacity, actively pursuing diversified income, adding one new outreach after the other at the institutional periphery, and gradually developing an entrepreneurial culture throughout most, if not all, of the basic departments that constitute the academic heartland. Equipped with a transformed infrastructure, the university was able to flex itself.

At Warwick, waiting for the government to come up with more money was seen as an option taken only by those who did not face reality. Spiraling downward into the muck of self-pity and low morale that was diffusing through so many British universities by years of bitter university-government relations was a road to be avoided at all costs During a decade and a half when British universities were having a very tough time, with more harsh medicine always in the offing, the university's self-steered success bolstered commitment and morale. Faculty had only to consider the plight of academic colleagues elsewhere in the UK, outside of the top half-dozen or so institutions, to become aware that Warwick's willingness to work with industry did not end up as a pact with the devil. Instead, industry's patronage, along with other second- and third-stream sources of income and program service, had become a crucial part of institutional viability. Income came from a plurality of sources the institution had to actively pursue in increasingly competitive settings. The financial base largely moved over to that part of the ledger where income streams differentiate institutions as they individually win or lose in obtaining research grants from private and public sources, pursue foreign students to garner fee income, sell contract-education courses and consultancy services, and attract conference and overnight guests to conference centers. In developing new sources of income the university has been out in front, at the cutting edge of a trend that affects UK universities generally and increasingly affects universities throughout developed and rapidly developing societies.

When the German Bertelsmann Foundation searched across Europe in late 1989 for the most impressive case of a progressive university, it chose Warwick as its winner. In a 1990 award, the foundation portrayed the university as "a model European university" that combined in an exemplary way "academic excellence and the imaginative generation of revenue." (Bertelsmann Foundation, 1990) The foundation hoped that by making the award to Warwick it would "help to promote understanding for appropriate and progressive university work both in Britain and in the rest of the world." The award was followed by a forum, for a largely German audience, that discussed the structure and administration of universities. Bertelsmann was interested in unfreezing the interlocked rigidities of the German university system (which have largely remained), and in calling attention to a model for all of Europe to consider. The award was appropriate. A half-decade later, Warwick remained an example second to none in Europe of university proactivity, one grounded in an aggressive attitude. In its brief to Bertelsmann, submitted in late 1989, Warwick stressed as the final element in its culture "a belief that attack is the best form of defence, or in university language, that optimism, some risk taking and a willingness to attempt new things represent a better policy than caution, cut-backs and academic conservatism." The university went on to point out that "the creation of a positive organizational culture is a lengthy process which cannot be achieved overnight," but that once you have it, a university has "a momentum" that carries it through difficult decisions and troubling times. (Shattock, 1989)

Underlying that culture and momentum we find many unique features of context, individual personality, and organizational process. But playing a large part are the five elements isolated in this study, elements common to Warwick and the four other universities described in the following chapters. Warwick serves as a vivid demonstration of these elements at work. As a leading case, it suggests strongly in itself that the five features we have uncovered are important pathways of university transformation at the end of the twentieth century. When we take Warwick seriously as a powerful model of the contemporary reformed university, we find university transformation built upon, even thoroughly dependent on, a strengthened administrative capacity, a buildup of discretionary funds, a vigorous periphery of outreach structures and programs, a willingness of heartland departments to join in the pursuit of new ventures and relationships, and, finally, a wrap-around entrepreneurial mentality that unites the university in a new direction of development and presents a distinctive outlook different from traditional modes.

Warwick teaches us much about what organizational changes enter into the making of entrepreneurial universities.

3

The Twente Response: Construction of a Dutch Entrepreneurial University

The University of Twente in The Netherlands is an excellent second place to pursue an analysis of entrepreneurial action in European universities. By the mid-1990s it too, like Warwick, had posted a strong reputation as a proactive university, one that caused rectors in other European countries to seek its advice on such matters as the promotion of technology transfer. It too is a young university that started up in the 1960s. Its early years, however, left much uncertainty about the future: life in the Dutch university system was not going to be easy. Responding to growing marginality, the institution set off in the early 1980s to fashion a more dependable character. It sought an institutional style that would lead to a distinctive niche in Dutch and European higher education.

Early Marginality

Officially created by the Dutch government in 1961, the Twente University of Technology (as it was then known) opened its doors to students in 1964, organized around three main faculties in mechanical, electrical, and chemical engineering. The university was expected to take up a place alongside two previously established technological universities: Delft, in existence since 1842, with a solidity gained from its age, tradition, size, and indeed location – the entire Rotterdam harbor was in its backyard; and Eindhoven, initiated just a few years before Twente in 1956 in the southern part of the country, with the advantage of a location close to a large firm, Philips, the Dutch electronics giant. Placed in this family, the new Twente was expected to link up with industry, even to draw some staff members from business firms. Equally important, it was also conceived as a regional university, located in eastern Holland not far from the German border, between the two small cities of Enschede and Hengelo, there to help the development of that particular region. (Maassen and van Buchem, 1990, pp. 55–58) Twente also took on from the start the special feature of a "campus university," with all academic, administrative, and service units brought together in one place, including some housing for students, faculty, and staff. Placed on a large estate, its campus nature was unique in Holland and highly unusual in all of Europe. Substituting for the urban life taken up by students and staff when faculties and departments of a university are spread around a city, Twente, technology and all, would have rolling hills, forests, lakes, and green fields.

The pastoral site, however, was situated in a region that was hardly a favorable environment for a university. Since its basic industry, textiles, had been collapsing for a long time as firms fled to cheap-labor locations in other countries, the Twente area was economically depressed. By the end of the 1960s the old textile mills, located squarely in the midst of the neighboring cities, were abandoned and largely useless structures, right down to empty smokestacks jutting into the sky that served as depressing daily reminders of jobs that had fled and economic base that had been lost. There was little existing industry to which the new university could connect. The economic environment was no more than a poor area much in need of major development.

Beyond the depressed economy, the Twente location was also marginal in the educational complex and cultural mentality of The Netherlands. Seen nationally as a region far from the governmental capital in The Hague, the great commercial centers of Amsterdam and Rotterdam, and the concentrated 50-mile corridor of high art and culture stretching along the Western region from Amsterdam and Haarlem to Leiden to The Hague to Delft, Rotterdam, and Dordrecht, the cultural setting was truly provincial. The Western heartland of high culture included the ancient, large comprehensive universities of Leiden (18,000 students in 1994), dating from the sixteenth century, and Utrecht (25,000) and Amsterdam (27,000), from the seventeenth, anchoring in the national system such later additions as the Free University of Amsterdam (14,000), not created until 1880, and the Erasmus University in Rotterdam (17,000), a new university of the 1970s. (Schutte, 1994, appendix A) Compared to life "over there" in the economic, political, and cultural heartland of Holland, the best the Enschede region could boast of, while ignoring the old smokestacks, was "a gentle farm region of gardens and streams."

The new university soon had a problem of size; it became in its first phase much smaller than planned. Beginning with a tiny enrollment of 200 in 1964, Twente was supposed to grow to 4,000 students by 1970. It got only 2,000.

Throughout the 1970s enrollment continued to be troublesome; in 1978, only 600 entering freshmen showed up and total enrollment was still less than 4,000. Income was similarly a threat: low enrollment meant low income from state finance based considerably on student numbers. And costs were too high on a campus built to be residential. Then, too, from the oil crisis of the early 1970s onward, the Dutch government got into the habit of cutting university budgets. Concerns were increasingly raised in the system at large about the costs of "too many universities" – or at least "too many faculties and programs." By the early 1980s the minister of education and science was explicitly indicating "that it was necessary, because of budgetary and other reasons, to close down a number of faculties and programs in Dutch institutions." (Maassen and van Buchem, 1990, p. 60)

The Dutch student culture of the late 1960s and the 1970s was notably unfriendly to a university planned to emphasize technology and orient itself to industry. Student attitudes in Holland and elsewhere in Europe were at a high point of anti-industry sentiment. Traditional preferences leaned toward the humanities and the social sciences and toward law and professional fields that led to employment in government and nonengineering professions. In 1970, 60 percent of entering students in the Dutch university system chose fields in the social sciences and humanities; this number increased by 1985 to 66 percent, with the humanities the great gainer, moving upward from 11 to 18 percent. Law was popular, increasing from 14 to 16 percent, and in itself drew as many students as all the engineering fields combined. Engineering at 15 and science at 11 percent only comprised about one-quarter of entering students in 1970 and less in 1985, falling to 14 and 8 percent. (Frijhoff, 1992, p. 501) A Dutch authority remarked that: "compared to other countries of Northern Europe, the proportion of students in the social sciences is in the Netherlands 5 to 20 percent higher, whereas that of the exact sciences is significantly lower . . . the highly developed welfare state . . . demands huge numbers of graduates from behavioral sciences and education, especially among women." (p. 501)

The campus setting in the early years was also hardly the asset in attracting students that British and American observers might readily assume. It ran contrary to the long-established understanding in Holland and in Europe generally that university students, declared mature in all respects by virtue of their university status, would live in big-city neighborhoods and make their way as best they could to lectures and classes in buildings spread around the metropolis. The campus idea took a bit of getting used to, and this feature was for a time as much an obstacle as an advantage in attracting students. Dutch students had to give up the delights of city life for the unknown joys of a pastoral setting.

Only a few years after this new university got underway, the moment of the participatory ("flower-power") university arrived fast and struck hard in the Dutch university system. As a response to strident student demands that spread across European countries after the 1968 Paris uprising, that the students together with nonacademic staff and junior faculty should share in the governance of the universities with the senior professors, at all levels, Holland as well as West Germany enacted laws and decrees in the early 1970s that forced tripartite representation in elected university councils from among the ranks of faculty, students, and support staff. (Daalder, 1982) Dutch society was in a new mood of rebellion against established élites with their quietly-passed-around prerogatives; and the universities, dominated by small numbers of chaired professors, also appeared to be structured for privilege. The universities were also beginning their march into expanded access – mass higher education – and as the ranks of junior staff rapidly grew, they too became unhappy with professorial dominance. Much was out of sorts: central government sharply intervened. The old university structure of dual governance by a board of regents (curatoren) and an academic senate was abolished. In its place was put a university council, largely composed of elected representatives from the three internal constituencies, and a much smaller (five to three member) executive board, composed of both elected and appointed members. The 1970 University Government Reorganization Act also spelled out in considerable detail the composition and intended functioning of internal faculties and new departmentlike units. The Act was indeed drastic, arguably the most extreme response in Europe to the student activism of the day. As aptly put by Hans Daalder, it was "in many ways a unique experiment in revolution from above, in response to student activism from below . . . " (1982, p. 174)

Student activism was relatively light at the new Twente: the activism was centered (as virtually everywhere else in the world) in the humanities and social sciences. Strident discord in Amsterdam did not produce similar levels of outcry in Enschede. But the drastic government response – the "revolution from above" – did have lasting effects: the new structure of a broadly elected central council, based on principles of participatory democracy, together with a small administrative board – with similar structures down the line – became an arrangement during the 1970s and early 1980s that stressed broad involvement rather than steering. Extended participation in elected councils meant lengthy and contentious deliberation. Fair shares were important to the various factions, especially in a society that deeply valued homogeneity and equity. A favorite saying claimed that "ordinary is extraordinary enough." Assertive leadership by rectors or small cadres of administrators and faculty was subordinated to participatory patterns. Later amendments (1986) to the revolutionary law of 15 years earlier sought to both reduce the number of council and board members and to increase the formal powers of the boards (Schutte, 1994, Appendix B); it was not until 1995, however, that the Dutch government finally found the will and the way to fully reverse the 1970 decree, leaving the matter of governance bodies to the individual universities. By then, those inside the universities had long worked out their own accommodations, with administrative and faculty expertise slowly given greater weight.

By 1980, as a result of all that happened and did not happen in its first 15 years, Twente had a serious problem of systemic marginality in Dutch higher education. Small in size and limited in scope, located "over there" in a depressed province, avoided rather than sought after by students, placed near the bottom of the totem pole in reputation and power among Dutch universities, vulnerable to financial crisis from government budget cuts, and uncommonly subject to rumors that some of its faculties or even the university as a whole might be closed down, the university faced a fundamental problem: how to escape from a weak, even quite threatening, institutional position. Were there pathways to be explored that would first of all guarantee survival, then lead on to healthy viability, and, finally, establish substantial status as a European university? The Twente response was to move sharply into a second stage of development that would in a decade or so produce a very different organization. Beginning in the early 1980s, the institution embarked on an overall bootstrap effort to make itself a larger, stronger, more self-reliant university, come what may in a turbulent environment of budget cuts and undependable student demand.

The Twente Takeoff

During the difficult years of the 1970s, several uncoordinated steps were taken to offer new programs that might attract students, increase income, and build faculty. Here the university was helped by the fact that from the outset, "unlike the other two universities of technology, it was designed to become a 'real' university with at least two academic cores: engineering and applied social sciences." (Maassen and von Buchem, 1990, p. 58) Toward building the second core, a faculty of business administration was set up in 1972, one in public administration was established in 1976, and a program in educational technology was developed in the late 1970s. On the applied science side, biomedical technology moved ahead with a research emphasis, and several established faculties gave birth to a new one in "informatics and computer sciences." What was lacking, however, in a setting where participation had triumphed over administrative leadership, was initiative at the center: "Some of those [above] steps were initiated by the faculties, and some were offered by the national government. The governing board of the university, however, lagged behind in this matter and initiated few of the necessary activities." (p. 59) What the university needed were more coordinated steps to hasten its evolution from an "education university," with only a minor profile in research activity, to a "research university." Research had international standing: it was what great European universities did. Research could also be a means of expanding income, attracting and increasing faculty in new and established fields, and diversifying the institutional reach to prospective students.

What steps were needed? The five elements identified in this study tell much of the story. We shall pursue them as they interact, first by briefly setting forth the role played by a strengthened administrative core, a new, strongly asserted institutional idea, and a new budget system. Then, by exploring the build-up of a new developmental periphery and the stimulation of the academic heartland, we follow the spread of entrepreneurship throughout the university.

Foremost, major change was instigated at Twente by a *strengthened administrative core*. The central administrative board had been relatively weak during the 1970s. Participation of all parties was the norm, and a large elected council guarded its dominating responsibilities. The subordinate posture of the five-person (later three-person) central board changed remarkably when two strong personalities, one elected and one appointed, assumed office, with the battle cry that "problems were opportunities," and set to work to lead a transforming effort. One was Harry Van den Kroonenberg, professor of mechanical engineering, who served a three-year term as rector between 1979 and 1982, then went formally off for a term, and then returned for a second between 1985 and 1988. The other was Erik Bolle, a mathematician who came from outside the university to serve during these years as administrative director, directly in charge of finance and planning. Van den Kroonenberg became in effect the man with an idea; Bolle the man who could plan and take the university onto a new financial footing. (Maassen and van Buchem, 1990, pp. 59–63) They were joined by Harry Fekkers, who served as head of a planning office and brought a new planning mentality and capability. This small group, exercising much central initiative, first developed a five-year plan, then instituted a decentralized budget scheme, and then moved by the end of the '80s into a second more sophisticated institutional plan for the 1990s, which sought to more precisely define a transformed character.

—*The institutional idea* put in place was the notion that Twente would become "the entrepreneurial university." A public figure and imposing speaker, Van den Kroonenberg took the case to the national government, business, and the general public, acting as "the ambassador of the university," that Twente was or soon would be decidedly different from the classical comprehensive universities and from what the institution had been during its early years of struggle. It now would become aggressively proactive, initiating new forms of contact with industry, city and regional government, and community groups; it would diligently serve national need and cooperate internationally. Keeping the concept simple, Van den Kroonenberg used the idea of "the entrepreneurial university" to help create a new public image that would "open windows" to national industry and local government, always emphasizing a "continuous flow of knowledge to society, not only by graduates, but also through an active transfer of science and technology directly into enterprises." (Maassen and van Buchem, 1991, p. 61) This theme, with its direct business overtones and its promise of strong ties to industry, was vigorously pushed at a time when it was an unpopular approach. Some faculty members, much aghast, felt obliged to point out that "we are an academic organization," not a business firm.

But this initial concept later transformed into an organizational culture. At the outset, it was only an idea, in and by itself a rhetorical statement. If it were to carry the day, it would need much sustained implementation. An administrative core devoted to the idea and to the difficult task of defining organizationally what it meant could be only the first of its moorings. The new idea and its initial supporting administrative cadre would need plenty of assistance from other organizational components.

A changed *budgetary system* became a critical component. Stimulated considerably during the 1981–1988 period by Eric Bolle, Twente devised an early form of decentralized budgeting now known around the world under such titles as lump-sum, cost-center, and responsibility-center budgeting. Rather than specify internal allocations within numerous large and small budget categories, an overall sum of money would be granted to basic units such as faculties, departments, and research centers. The operational units would be encouraged to raise additional funds. Such lump-sum budgeting can be a major shock to faculty and staff. All that freedom to raise and spend! But then all that responsibility to make hard choices among desired expenditures, and all that unit accountability to work within university parameters and national standards. Twente was strict in this regard: it went to "full-cost accounting" in which virtually all service/support costs, such as use of office space and of the computer center, were charged to the basic units.

What lump-sum budgeting at Twente did was help fix attention within basic units on cost control *and* on enhancing income from a number of sources, widening the financial base beyond ministry-of-education core support. (Schutte, 1994) The latter, known in The Netherlands as the first flow of funds, was heavily dependent on student numbers, at the point of entry or their overall enrollment; the amount was influenced later by the addition of an "output measure," the number of students completing the first major degree in a satisfactory span of time. Here basic units could increase income by managing to attract more students and to graduate them on time. Basic institutional grants also contained funds earmarked for research support.

The second flow of funds consisted of income from money the government places in the hands of national research councils; in Holland they were grouped in the Netherlands Organization for the Advancement of Scientific Research (NWO). This type of income depended, as it did at Warwick, on success in competing for research grants. The third flow consisted of income raised from all other sources, largely through contract research, contract education, and consultancy. The three largest contributors to this stream at Twente became, in order, industry, the European Union, and other governmental ministries. Here entrepreneurship could pay the greatest dividends: by providing additional sums of money *and* by enhancing budgetary discretion at university and basic unit levels.

Twente worked hard to enhance income from sources other than governmental core support. As late as 1980 the university was almost totally dependent on core support, at about 96 percent of total income. During the 1980s, this support fell 22 percentage points, to about 74 percent, while third stream sources increased from less than 5 to over 20 percent.

TABLE 3–1
Sources of Financial Support, University of Twente 1970–1995
(millions of Dutch guilders)

	Core Support		Research Councils		All Other Sources*		Total	
Year	Amount	Percent	Amount	Percent	Amount	Percent	Amount	Percent
1970	37.5	93	**	-	2.9	7	40.4	100
1975	89.5	94	**	-	5.6	6	95.1	100
1980	134.4	96	**	-	5.4	4	139.8	100
1985	155.7	85	3.9	2	23.4	13	183.0	100
1990	177.0	74	13.0	5	50.6	21	240.6	100
1995	233.5	76	10.4	3	63.7	21	307.6	100

*Includes tuition and fees

**Unknown: estimated to be less than 2 percent of the total, based on 1985 figure of 2 percent.

Source: trend data provided by Michiel Van Buchem, Deputy Secretary, University of Twente

The figures in table 3 clearly indicate that beyond the major provision for research made within the first line, much research-based and highly discretionary funding was achieved by increased capacity to generate income from non-traditional sources as well as from research councils. As they generated income, "contract research" and "contract education" became budgetary components of "the entrepreneurial university." In Holland's higher education system, a yield of 20 percent or more in the total budget from third-stream sources pointed to successful entrepreneurship. Central administrators pointed out in interview that Twente's contract income, as a share of all revenues, was by far the largest of all Dutch universities.

When third-stream figures were viewed as income added beyond the base of core support, then 20 percent became 27–28 percent, and approximated one-third when small sums from research councils were included. Such non-core additional shares of income are minor when compared to the extreme situation we observed at Warwick, which at the cutting-edge of change in the UK totaled over 50 percent. But in the Holland of the 1990s, Twente authorities felt that "there is a limit to the increase of turnover and profit of contract research, contract education and consultancy. We estimate the balance to be between one-quarter and one-third of the state budget, since exceeding this limit would make the university too much dependent [on] industry and extra-governmental income." (Schutte, 1994, p. 19) But "profit" clearly accrued to faculties and departments. And the central board in one form or another could reserve some of all income for its own use and then invest in new programs or selectively support older ones that ought to go forward but were and are unable to pay for themselves. The board adopted the habit of allocating all income it received to faculties and departments and then clawing-back over 30 percent as a charge for central services: "We do apply a 'tax' to the units in the sense that the total budget is allocated to the faculties, and then a specific part of the budget (1994: approx. 32%) is deduced to cover the central services, non-normative allocations and projects." (Schutte, 1994, p. 15)

As the three elements of institutional idea, strengthened administrative core, and discretionary funding base developed in an interactive fashion they fed into and were strengthened in their effects by a growing *developmental periphery*. As we saw at Warwick, the periphery of a university can be difficult to define. Some basic departments may readily reach out across formal university boundaries; new units that start out in a peripheral location may in time work their way into core standing; and some academic units such as research centers, cast in a nondepartmental mold, may be seen as half-way between core and periphery. At Twente, the development of a much expanded periphery took two main forms: a true periphery of outreach units; and a semiperiphery of outward-looking, problem-solving research centers reflecting faculty interests even though they sprung up outside departments. In the first, more precise form, new units and programs have developed at Twente that stretch across traditional university boundaries to link up with industrial firms, professional associations, and the community. Here the main evolutionary story lies in industrial liaison. Of special note in the 1990s has been the development of a "privatized" business school that remains operationally a part of the university while formally constituted to be outside its rules and regulations.

In its effort to reach out to industry, Twente made an early start on devising a "structured relationship" with small and medium companies, primarily in the local province. As a Van den Kroonenberg idea, the university established a "Transferpunt" office in 1979 to explore ways to link up with industry and increase third-stream income. (Maassen and van Buchem, 1990) The ministry was reducing the mainline budget; the region was demanding the university help out in economic development; and the institution desperately needed income. During the early 1980s, Van den Kroonenberg did some "piloting": he helped his own mechanical engineering students to establish their own firms. This led in 1984 to the initiation of a program known as TOP (Temporary Entrepreneurial Placements) designed to support "prospective entrepreneurs who want to start their business from an entrepreneurial university." (University of Twente, 1995b)

Hitting squarely at the problem of technology transfer from university to small and medium-size enterprises – a more difficult process than working with sophisticated large firms – TOP conceived of such transfer taking place by means of graduates situated in new spin-off companies ("starters"), as well as by means of the normal output of graduates to existing companies ("absorbers"). TOP, located in a new office known as TRD (Transfer, Research and Development), strived to stimulate graduates and researchers "to start their own knowledge-intensive company." Assistance in the "incubation-phase" would be important. As the program became worked out in the 1980s, the university offered an interest-free loan, office space and connection to a university research group, advice and training in preparing a business plan and working out management, marketing, and financing strategies, and even in time a faculty mentor and courses on how to become an entrepreneur.

TOP has been open to graduates of other Dutch universities, as well as Twente graduates, and to people from industry. Financing for TOP began with an initial five-year grant from the Dutch Ministry of Economic Affairs (1984–1989) and then was assumed by a revolving fund after 1990 based on repayment of loans and some support from a European Union fund. The goal of about 15 yearly awards has been realized in the decade since 1984. By 1995, the TRD office could claim that 200 places had been awarded to individuals, in 160 new enterprises that created over 1,100 new jobs. The failure rate among these new firms was only 20 percent. Counting new firms assisted by the university from 1976 onward, the university could claim by 1995 over 250 spin-offs. The TOP-assisted firms ranged across such specialties as mechanical engineering and design, microelectronics/optics, environmental engineering, international marketing, and organizational management; about one-half were cast as production units, the other as consulting firms.

The university was able by the 1990s to depict a three-stage organizational flow in the formation and continuation of the new enterprises. In the first phase individuals and new firms initially sponsored by TOP reside for a year or so in some part of the university. In a second stage survivors then take up residence in the Business and Technology Center (BTC) – an "incubator center" – supported by firms and local government, adjacent to the campus. Then, when time and growth dictates, the fledgling firm could move on from the BTC to the Twente Business and Science Park that had been gradually developing adjacent to both campus and the center. The science park developed quite informally; in 1995, it still did not have a headquarters office. Officials at the university portray the TOP scheme and its follow-on connections as a "step-by-step, organic-growth model," rather than as a planned development. The science park received a major boost in the mid-1990s when a major branch of Ericsson, the giant Swedish electrical firm, moved in, giving the park an "anchor tenant." Ericsson apparently saw Twente as a well-located, growing high-tech area. Local government had set aside many lots of open land for further science-park development, all close to the university. Bottom-up networking seemed well underway: for example, some 80 high-tech firms formed a Technology Group Twente as a society for discussion of problems and exchange of ideas; an Entrepreneur House had sprung up. And in 1996 the science park clearly entered a period of rapid growth. A comprehensive plan was designed, more high-tech firms were moved in, and a new railway station located directly at the park was completed. In a related move, the university had under construction a "Da Vinci" Science and Technology Museum.

A new program, TOS, developed in 1988 as a spin-off idea from the TOP format. Temporary Support Spin-Offs was intended to extend the spin-off idea from young entrepreneurs to more experienced people already employed in firms. TOS would start up "faster growing spin-off ventures by linking spin-off ideas from industry to experienced entrepreneur[s] and UT-research group[s] for further development and commercialization of the product." (University of Twente, 1995b) But many problems befell the TOS program. Its staff learned the hard way that if firms are asked to nominate individuals who might be spun-off to work on an idea, the firms might readily suggest people they wanted to eliminate. It was better to ask for promising ideas, have a wide range of individuals apply for the general program, then match the most promising individuals with the best ideas, and then go back to the companies, and the European Community, for funds. TOS has proven to be a lot of work for small results. After 50 worthwhile spin-off ideas were extracted from 35 companies, just 13 spin-off ventures were generated; from these nine still existed in the mid-1990s. Nevertheless, the university pointed to "indirect results" gained in increasing the interaction between it, established industry, and TOP-like small companies, which helped to construct a stronger local network.

In 1995–1996, TRD and its constituent programs, frequently running into deficits, were made part of a larger outreaching administrative unit. A new Liaison Group (LG) was conceived to have three major components: a section for "Research Programs and Regional Development" – the former TRD; a second part, "Permanent and Post-Initial Education," for contract education, largely continuing education courses for professionals; and, as the third piece, "International Cooperation." Early on the new unit pointed to the accumulated experience of its predecessors since the early 1980s in "technology transfer, spin-off creation and academic entrepreneurship." In such areas, and in relationships with business centers, technology centers, and science parks, LG sees itself as "an important actor (on behalf of the university) in the regions of Twente, Friesland, and Gelderland," three areas that together cover most of northeastern and northern Holland. (University of Twente, 1996) The university increasingly sees its direct outreach as a national one, especially to the least-developed half of the country. It has expanded its sphere from an initial local base to a broad area.

Twente programs have spread increasingly to other countries in Europe. In the mid-1990s, Twente officials were busy explaining their TRD-type operation to German university administrators, European Union program administrators, and interested officials in Eastern Europe, Latin American, and South Africa. How to do "industrial liaison" effectively and in an academically appropriate way had become a primary issue. An early start on an idea whose time had come by the 1990s had given Twente 15 years of experience in working out, through much trial-and-error, an implementing infrastructure.

Twente has also taken the highly unusual step of "privatizing" a business school within its midst, all the better to put MBA and executive-training programs in a tub-on-its-own-bottom type of administrative arrangement, a separate operation from the first-degree work in business studies supported by mainline governmental funding. The "private" school, known as the Twente Business School (TSM), started up in the late 1980s as a major spin-off from the established faculty in management studies. It operates "a commercialized MBA" degree through four different self-supporting full and part-time MBA programs, on and off campus. TSM runs executive-training programs and also arranges for business and professional associations to bring their own training programs to campus, renting conference space and sports facilities (TSM, 1995). Unique for Holland, the school accepts only students who have taken their first degree in engineering or science. TSM does not need its own faculty: rather, it draws its teaching staff from the regular business-studies faculty, the faculty of other Dutch universities and polytechnics, and directly from business firms and other outside employers. Beginning in 1993, TSM (renamed the TSM Business School) became a three-university arrangement, a "cooperative venture" of the universities of Twente, Groningen, and Eindhoven that ranged up and down the eastern region of the country. It is, to say the least, thoroughly entrepreneurial.

Beyond the new infrastructure evolved for a structured relationship with industry, to promote technology transfer, and the extended outreach achieved in privatized business courses, Twente developed an unusual third major type of outreach in the form of an "intrapreneurial" component. The concept and formation of "the intrapreneurial university" developed in the mid-1980s when the initiative-taking central board found that the public law under which the university operated stood in the way of exploring and developing new activities. The imaginative answer was to establish a sort of private enterprise within the university, which could operate under civic law. As put by Maassen and van Buchem (1990, pp. 66–67), when "the provisions of Dutch public law did not allow the university to undertake certain entrepreneurial activities . . . Twente dealt with this impediment by setting up, in 1985, a private enterprise called Technopolis Twente. The secretary of Twente was appointed as its president, and the members of the university governing board constitute its corporate board. Its main purpose is to offer a structure in which activities can be developed as spin-offs of regular university tasks such as research, teaching, and social service." Technopolis Twente, later renamed UT-Extra, has been operating as a Dutch foundation that could spin-off specific working companies: "In this structure every industrial spin-off can be accommodated. Since we make use of limited companies we are able to profit from all stimulation regulations, bounty systems, grants and state aids that are possible in The Netherlands, ranging from investment grants and wage aids to development credits." (Schutte, 1994, p. 27)

Under this broad foundation mechanism, the university has been able to accomplish the following: build a hotel on campus, the International

Conference and Study Centre – on ground owned by the Ministry of Education! – by using two limited companies for construction and management; construct an office building, the Office Centre Technopolis, to rent out space that serves contract research activities; build a day-care center; start an Educational Computer Consortium for the development of educational software/courseware, an enterprise later sold to a private firm; and found a Business Technology Group, to further the work of the chemical engineering department in developing countries, later sold off to its leading participants. (Schutte 1994, p. 27)

UT-Extra exemplifies entrepreneurial attitude and spirit. Its formation tested the limits of what could be done under traditional rules and reflected a determination to find a procedure for getting around state constraints when they stood in the way. It meant risking scarce income on new ventures. And it entailed hazarding the ire of traditional patrons by bypassing their expectations and dictates. This Dutch experiment was risky as well as innovative.

Much has also happened at Twente in an expanded semiperiphery of research centers, nondepartmental units that readily reached across traditional boundaries as they built directly outward from the basic faculties and departments, enlarging the circumference of the university. Often interdisciplinary, they typically drew on faculty and students from more than one department and even from more than one faculty, as, for example, institutes for biomedical technology and "production, logistics, and operational management." Dutch universities are free to initiate research centers, to encourage their development. National legislation in 1986 gave formal status to "recognized centers" of unusual merit, with earmarked financial support. Twente had seven centers on the approved list in the mid-1990s.

A good example of the development of a Twente research center is its Center for Higher Education Policy Studies (CHEPS) which in 1995–1996 had been underway for 12 years. The major budget cut of the 1980s, laboriously being implemented beginning in 1981, prompted the minister in charge of higher education in 1983 to suggest that the universities study themselves. Quick off the mark, Eric Bolle seized the opportunity – "Twente can do it" – made a bid right off, and was rewarded with a ministerial, initial five-year grant of 500,000 guilders a year, to be matched by the university. Two years of discussion within, particularly by faculty members drawn from the fields of education, business, and public policy, led to the start-up of a new center in 1984–1985. After one year of temporary direction by an administrator, Frans van Vught, a young scholar in the Faculty of Public Policy, with a background in policy analysis and urban planning, became director and remained in this position until 1996, when he became the university's rector. The center started out with four "researchers" – professional level appointments – drawn from political science, economics, education, and methodology and statistics.

The center has operated under five-year review by the university: in 1995, judged to be quite successful, it was on its third approved cycle. After the initial five-year government grant, it has been supported by institutional money and what it raises from outside sources, mainly from contract research. In the mid-1990s, such research carried out for the ministry contributed a fourth of income. "Policy work" has been done for such diverse outside agencies as the World Bank, UNESCO, and the South African government. It has done much contract work for the European Union and has been heavily involved in the efforts to restructure Russian higher education. Like most other UT research centers, CHEPS has an interdisciplinary base, here the original three sponsoring faculties. It has also increasingly taken on "an international appearance," encouraged both by the ministry and the university.

CHEPS became a recognized national center of excellence in the mid-1990s. The national government gave it this special formal status along with three other centers at UT. Having grown to over twenty researchers, including seven or more Ph.D. students working on dissertations, CHEPS by 1995 was the major research house of its kind in the world, combining domestic practical projects with basic research in comparative higher education. Its practical outreach activities include consulting with governments and universities on such contemporary issues as "assessment" and "quality assurance," and serving as the secretariat for international associations of university administrators and higher education researchers, for example, the European Association for Institutional Research (EAIR) and the Consortium of Higher Education Researchers (CHER). Its scholarly contribution has been exhibited in a rapidly growing body of volumes and papers which, particularly on policy issues, span not only the countries of Europe but also reach as far afield as the United States, Japan, and Australia.

The final enabling element in our discussion is the very critical matter of an ongoing stimulation of *the academic heartland*. Twente responded to its marginality and questionable viability, still so evident at the end of the 1970s, by promoting a process of organizational parturition (or what in business might be called "building from core competencies"). Here new faculties, fields of study, and programs were developed as new combinations out of existing units. As indicated earlier, the 1970s saw developments of this kind in the birth of a new faculty in informatics and computer sciences and a program in educational technology. At the end of the 1980s, however, central administration and concerned faculty still saw vulnerability in Twente's limited scope as a technological university and its peripheral geographic location. The vulnerability resided in questionable capacity to attract students in a dependable, ongoing fashion. The response was to "broaden our scope." Three new programs were started between 1988 and 1992. One, civil engineering and management, trained project managers in the building industry; this required some investment in the Faculty of Mechanical Engineering together with expertise drawn from management studies. A second, computer science and management, later to be "business information technology," drew upon core units in computer science and business management. A third program start-up was "communication," fashioned from established units in education, philosophy, and public policy and public administration. All three programs were interdisciplinary, and were meant to tap into student interest. By 1995 the three programs enrolled over 10 percent of the student population. Their emergence and evident contribution was an important form of university responsiveness to changing student and labor market interests. Even though they too become institutionalized in time, with personnel sunk costs, such programs were also easier to initiate and discontinue than were faculties and departments. Their construction and use became a form of university adaptability.

Such internal experimentation has become a habit at Twente. Efforts to work out new programs between faculties are praised as internal entrepreneurship. In the mid-1990s, the faculties of mechanical engineering and electrical engineering were working with an education center on campus to devise a new curriculum that would be at least 40 percent "project-oriented." There, teachers teach and students learn by involvement in projects – an attractive possibility devised to increase student motivation and learning, modeled in western Europe by the University of Aalborg in Denmark. The new program in communications sought to hook up with business. The connection between civil engineering and business came to include preparation for the transportation industry as well as construction. Information science and business education had become BIT, a program combining business, information, and technology. And the university felt in 1995 that there was need "to further diversify the teaching programs." In 1996, the university was exploring potential new programs in telematics, medical technology, and the management of medical facilities. Quality was not a problem: Twente was getting good evaluations in one field after another. But with the government cutting back anew on student allowances, especially on transportation costs, location could again hurt, for then students stay closer to home to conserve costs, and Twente's nationwide draw of students would decline. Such are the joys of dependence on the vagaries of national systemwide policies and procedures.

New organizational units for the support of research continued to multiply. In the 1990s, Dutch higher education entered the realm of organized graduate schools for systematic work in doctoral programs by creating interuniversity "research schools," approved by the academy of science. Soon the university was participating in eight such emerging clusters, with three headquartered on campus, causing central administrators to feel "we are doing quite well" at this, with more than "our share" of such schools. Research centers and research schools are where new developments on campus particularly come together with the traditional heartland. In this domain, driven so much by faculty interest, "periphery" readily becomes "core," or the next thing to it. But whether viewed as periphery or core, the research units and the developmental offices discussed above add greatly to the university's outreach efforts and to its flexibility.

Back in the *strengthened administrative core* of Twente, the task of creating a true entrepreneurial university proved to be an unceasing business. Changing the budgeting process has been particularly difficult, and procedures continued to evolve in the late 1980s and the 1990s. Additionally, much smoothing of the way has been called for in relationships between the central board and the faculties and departments, particularly when the national government cut its support. Then the central board was forced to pass along the bad news either with reduced equal-share allocations or selective cuts; *and* to insist that the basic units were now responsible for coming up with still more of their "own" income.

A new group of central administrators took over: Frits Schutte, who succeeded Erik Bolle as administrative director in 1988, took over the budgeting task. He continued through 1996 to play an important role within a collective leadership. Two professors, Jos de Smit (1988–1992) and Theo Popma (1992–1996), who served as rectors after Van den Kroonenberg, believed strongly in the changing character of the university and worked to extend and consolidate it. During their years in office leadership became somewhat more diffused. The deanships in the faculties have become more time-consuming, responsible positions, even full-time posts, and a cadre of administrative directors serving at the faculty level have assumed major responsibilities under the dictates of lump-sum budgeting. The faculties have been responsible for this type of budgeting to their constituent departments. Especially when government cuts university budgets, faculties then feel especially caught in the middle between central board and departments. What appeared to be happening at Twente was an evolution toward a larger overall management group that would associate the deans more closely with central decision making. (This change did happen in early 1997, as this book was under preparation. The new rector, Frans A. Van Vught, installed a new "Management Team" consisting of the three members of the central board and all the deans.)

Most important, by the mid-1990s the initial simple *idea* of an entrepreneurial university had not only developed structural footing but had also been elaborated into a much broader ideology that took up residence in the many faculties and departments as an embracing culture. The university's *Strategic Plan 1991*, replacing a 1987 plan (and in 1995 not yet succeeded by another), spelled out in detail its "profile and mission." What did the University of Twente (UT) really mean when it gave itself the title of "the entrepreneurial university?"

UT is *entrepreneurial*: this is used in two senses, referring both to an "attitude" and to "doing business on one's own account and at one's own risk."

The UT wishes to adopt an entrepreneurial approach in the sense of being daring, unafraid of taking on things which are difficult, risky or bold. The UT aims for this attitude at all levels: in teaching, in research, but also in the way in which decisions are made and the university is administered. This is what the UT primarily means by "being entrepreneurial." It does not however alter the fact that the UT will not pass up the opportunity of taking an entrepreneurial approach in the second sense of the word (i.e., of doing business and making money), if this means that it can contribute to its main responsibility, that of being a university. (University of Twente, 1991, p. 2)

Beyond this broad statement, after a decade of implementation, the university could assert with considerable warrant a fascinating set of claims about its character. UT had become (University of Twente, 1991, p. 16; Schutte, 1994):

– "the two-core university": a place for applied science and applied social science, uniquely linked, a combination that neither the other two technological universities nor the comprehensive universities offered as foci of organization.

– "the campus university": a place with student housing and some faculty and staff quarters set among virgin forest groves, green lawns, and lakes, leading to "living, working, and enjoying recreation on a single site" and to "a financially self-reliant campus organization."

– "the responsible university": a place committed to the economic and cultural development of its region, and to cooperative arrangements with other educational institutions in providing higher vocational, continuing, and university education for all of northeast Netherlands.

– "the university without frontiers": a place always working hard to strengthen its international character, through international research institutes and promotion of international student mobility.

– "the focused university": a place that aims for an "appropriate depth of coverage in a limited number of fields across their full range." Twente had learned that, even in a small university, sharp selection of subjects can offer critical mass in the fields selected – a follow-up of the two-core idea.

– "the flexible university": a place that achieves uncommon versatility through ongoing reform of its governance, strengthened channels of accountability, internal redeployment of personnel, and, especially, creative use of resources, where "the incomes resulting from contract funding are sources of independent means which can be spent freely. This of course greatly increases the UT's flexibility."

The initial idea, in short, became a profile of connected beliefs, an unfolding set of relatively unified definitions of institutional character, along with the usual claims of "high quality student-centered teaching" and "high quality research," the latter tilted toward "strategic" and "multi-disciplinary."

In its fleshed-out later form the idea had spread across the basic units, producing a fully *stimulated heartland*. The entrepreneurial attitude could be found in virtually every department; it was particularly strongly expressed in the research centers. As put in an interview in 1994 by a professor who had had a role both at the center and at the faculty level, "an entrepreneurial university is a university of entrepreneurs." To this, we can add, of entrepreneurial units. Although departments will always vary in income-raising vigor and efficient internal administration, all had to join into the spirit of the overall change. All were "cost centers," even "profit centers," in which inattentive administration, or unwillingness to seek income, would become self-destructive behavior.

Among the basic units at Twente there are virtually ideal types of how best to combine the new with the old, the entrepreneurial spirit and close relationship to industry with the traditional regard for basic research and major standing in the world of research universities. One such role model, the Faculty of Chemical Technology, has achieved a heady mixture of virtues. Its faculty and budget size make it the largest of the ten faculties. In 1995, permanent academic staff numbered over 50; nonpermanent staff over 150 full-time equivalent. Nearly 700 students were enrolled in first degree programs of about 11 sub-departments; some 110 to 120 advanced students (formally "research workers") were pursuing the Ph.D. and served as the main labor force for research activity grounded in 10 to 12 research institutes and newly created "research schools" in which the faculty participated. The faculty had its own stable administrative core, an elected dean who was on his third three-year term and an administrative director who had been in his post for 10 years, on indefinite appointment, and who headed an administrative office of over 50 people. About two-thirds of income in the faculty's overall budget came from the first stream, income from third-stream research contracts was much the larger item in the remaining one-third, amounting to about one-fourth of the total budget. For research purposes alone, 60 percent of income came from industry. A larger number of Ph.D. students (40 percent) were supported in this fashion than by mainline institutional support (27 percent) or by the governmental research councils (33 percent). New young faculty had commonly both taken the Ph.D. and served in industry before coming to the university, gaining middle and senior rank appointments. (University of Twente, 1995a)

The faculty offers abundant evidence that it has firm ties to industry and that it values entrepreneurial activity in seeking research contracts. At the same time it places great value on basic research, publication, and a world-class reputation. Citation analysis of research publications in the field of chemical technology, as reported by the faculty from analyzes presented in *Science Watch* in the mid-1990s, placed Twente second in the world, following the Massachusetts Institute of Technology (MIT). Senior staff in this faculty stress that "quality recruitment is everything," that is, quality as judged by traditional academic criteria. Movement has been "up-market" in academic reputation, even as ties to industry become stronger and the faculty becomes a place for entrepreneurs. The faculty was able to say, in a report prepared for a national quality assessment: "A worldwide recognition has been achieved within at least four areas. They comprise membranes, reactor concepts and modeling, supramolecular chemistry, and biomaterials. These areas are fine examples of integration of fundamental knowledge and technological aspects, and all of them are strongly interdisciplinary." (University of Twente, 1995a, p.1)

Not surprising, by the mid-1990s, the entrepreneurial attitude had taken hold among undergraduate and graduate students throughout the campus. The university sought to instill an attitude favorable to small and middle-size firms, even to emphasize to first-degree students that starting up one's own firm after graduation could be "a higher value in life" than going to work for a large corporation. In an age of corporate downsizing and decreasing lifetime employment, it could also be a highly prudent choice. The death of Fokker, a large firm highly symbolic of Dutch manufacturing greatness, drove home this point. In small firms, graduates could help rebuild the country's economic base.

Picking up on this approach, some Twente undergraduates, while still students, set up their own small firms or consulting services to earn money and gain experience in small-group enterprise. The central board, finding certain projects "too expensive to explore through regular administrative staff," farmed them out to hardworking and imaginative student groups they knew would be inexpensive to fund. When the board wanted to know more (for admission purposes) about what was happening in the upper secondary schools, including getting access to data the schools were not publicly sharing (on student numbers in different classes and programs), a student group did the research by sampling classes and programs and produced a useful report. Student clubs have been doing the new work of organizing an alumni at about 20 percent of the cost of using regular administrative staff. To engage in such efforts, the top students at Twente openly and self-consciously look for one another, "headhunting" for talent within their ranks.

*   *   *   *

The Twente of 1995 had become in all respects a far cry from the marginal institution of 1980. The less-than-viable 2,900 students of 1980 became over 7,300 a decade later. First degrees awarded shot up from less than 200 a year to over 600 in 1990 and then to reach over 1,000 in 1995. Advanced students increased from about 100 at the beginning of the 1990s to over 300 in 1990 and then to more than 600 in 1995; doctoral degrees jumped from 14 to 87 in the 15-year period. The faculty doubled in size during the 1980s, from about 500 to over 1,000. Supporting research personnel swelled to about 600. The faculty structure that gave birth to new interdisciplinary as well as disciplinary programs settled down to ten major building blocks: six on the science side, with the original three of mechanical, electrical, and chemical engineering joined by applied physics, applied mathematics, and computer science; and four largely located within the second focus, business administration/management studies, public administration and public policy, educational science and technology, and a faculty of "philosophy, technology, and society," the smallest by far at about 60 enrolled students. Large faculties with over 500 students each included the original three engineering fields and computer science, and then management studies and public administration, which had grown to be two of the three largest at 1,300 and 800 students respectively. When Frans A.

Van Vught, the head of CHEPS, was elected rector in 1996, Twente was ready for a rector drawn from the social sciences.

Conclusion

The faculties, departments, and research centers at Twente separately and together define operationally an elaborated idea of an entrepreneurial university. Located together on one campus, they are conceptually grouped around two substantive foci. They typically participate in interdisciplinary, interfaculty, and interuniversity programs; they commonly relate to outside enterprises, public and private; they commonly find flexibility in the fourth or more of their lump-sum budget they raise from such sources. They assume in miniature the character the university as a whole claims for itself, and thereby offer a crucial link in the interactive chain of formative elements.

The Twente University of 1996 could fairly claim that for over 15 years it "had turned problems into opportunities." It could justifiably claim that given its entrepreneurial attitude and somewhat flexible character it would go on doing so. Being something less than a fully comprehensive university turned out to have had major advantages. Institutional foci had thereby been somewhat easier to agree upon and highlight. Little involved in the humanities and pure social sciences, Twente has also had the good fortune to be less politicized then the Dutch comprehensive universities by the culture wars of the preceding quarter-century. With engineering modes of thought permeating the institution, it could appropriately claim an overall no-nonsense attitude, one that had spread among its social scientists. That attitude included a willingness to experiment with changes that might strengthen the institution.

But entrepreneurship and innovative character are not easily accepted matters in a university, especially one situated in a country where state-defined patterns applied across universities have until recently offered common thresholds of security. Such patterns were set in the larger context of national values that stressed individual and group equity and frowned upon assertive competitiveness. And the character that Twente assumed, it was clear by the mid-1990s, would provide no resting point. That character placed a heavy burden on organization, that is, on a capacity to go on developing new structures and orientations that meld the advantages of successful new programs with the advantages of old ones successfully brought forward to a new stage. And however entrepreneurial the new look, the institution still contained residues of prior periods. As one administrator put it, in pointing to phases of university development in Europe, the "professorial" university of forty years ago had been partially replaced by the "participatory university" of the post-1968 period, which had now partially given way to the "managerial university." The changes were never total; all three phases continue to exist in the current framework, adding to complexity and muddling institutional character.

But as difficult as entrepreneurial character has proven to be, especially in pushing hard against traditional collegial and participatory values, any return to the status quo ante was ruled out. On the pre-entrepreneurial road, Twente would have remained marginalized and vulnerable. Now, in the brief span of a decade and a half, it had become in important respects a self-confident place. Its entrepreneurship helped it to evolve toward industry, toward research, and toward advanced degrees. It was "less dependent on The Hague"; it had become "one of those places where things happen." It diffused useful patterns of organization to other universities in The Netherlands, elsewhere in Europe, and even among developing nations. As alliances among highly progressive universities began to form across Europe in the mid-1990s, the university was a leading actor. A new European Consortium of Innovative Universities held its first meeting at Twente in 1996.

In the retrospect of the late 1990s, the Twente takeoff of the 1980s had put it on the front end of a metamorphosis that had to come sooner or later to Dutch universities. Individually they would learn to assert an institutional self that would promote, and be promoted by, differentiation, selectivity, and competition. In a featured Opinion article in the London *Times Higher Education Supplement* (*THES*) in early 1996 (May 24, 1996), the president of Holland's ancient and august university, Leiden, stressed that the time had come for the universities of the country "to break with the Dutch policy of uniformity . . .," that detailed legislation and governmental financial control together with the sheer number of students had "leveled Dutch university education into drab uniformity. As in the bed of Procrustes, everything was reduced or stretched to the same size. Carried to the extreme, a situation could develop in which the government is frantically attempting to keep 13 identical universities open with only the minimum of resources." His own university for one, the president indicated, would now seek "to escape from the equality straitjacket." To strengthen the good, he maintained, Leiden would abandon the mediocre, choosing among activities to match constrained resources; it would exact higher requirements and recruit fewer students. "Fortunately" the state would now help "a university with ambition," for even "the minister has come to realize that it is necessary to stimulate differentiation and selectivity in the teaching provided by and research performed by the universities." The president of a second ancient university, Utrecht, had come to a similar view, stressing that with differentiation and selectivity there would now be more competition, a good thing. (*Science*, 1996, p. 693) As Dutch universities found they did not have the funds and the infrastructure to meet the ever-expanding demands of the day, entrepreneurial action seemed likely to become a more common feature.

What Twente has done to transform its character offers lessons in the possibilities of change in modern universities. It exemplifies to a high degree the common enacting elements identified in this study. An assertive, forward-looking self-concept, a strengthened administrative core, and a discretionary funding base had borne fruit organizationally in an extended developmental periphery and a much stimulated heartland. Academic basic units had become different from their counterparts in traditional university faculties and departments. If, at the outset, in the early 1980s the strengthened administrative core was the instigating element, 15 years later the extended periphery and the stimulated heartland had become the most important features in the changed institution. The firm ground of Twente's transformation is found in its infrastructure of entrepreneurial units.

4

The Strathclyde Phenomenon: Organizational Assertion of Useful Learning in Scotland

In 1996 the University of Strathclyde celebrated a bicentennial under the banner of "200 years of useful learning." A long evolutionary trail leading up to university status in the heady days of the 1960s lay behind that claim. The road early chosen was not one of classical learning and pastoral spires but of practical training in downtown workshops. No effort was made either to imitate Oxford or Cambridge or to hanker after the posture of an ancient Scottish university, not even to attempt to clone a nineteenth century British civic university. Instead, a mechanics' institute turned into a technical college that in time became a technological university. Development took place along a relatively low-status pathway, one that for almost two centuries left the institution outside the pale of the British university system. Its particular track would have been readily recognized on the continent, where engineering-centered universities had a regular place, but in Britain its historic definition left much to be desired.

The Institutional Antecedents

In the beginning there was John Anderson, a noted Scottish professor of the day who, decidedly vexed with the ways of traditional academics and students in his University of Glasgow, left sums in his will for the establishment of a training institution to be devoted to the practical arts for practical students. Anderson, and the tiny institute founded in his name, marked the beginning of a popular but marginal educational movement. Eric Ashby dates the origins of "the mechanics' institutes – one of the great educational movements in British history. . . to the 'anti-toga' lectures (open to the public) given by. . . the querulous and eccentric John Anderson" while he was serving for three decades as professor of natural philosophy at the University of Glasgow, the second largest of Scotland's four ancient universities. Scornful of his university peers, Anderson lectured to large numbers of "gardeners, painters, shopmen, porters, founders, bookbinders, barbers, tailors, potters, glassblowers, gunsmiths, engravers, brewers, and turners." (Ashby, 1958, p. 51; Kelly, 1957) A few years after the new institute was up and running, one George Birkbeck, a like-minded spirit, served as a professor who also enjoyed lecturing without fees to working men, and, upon migrating to London, used his experience in Glasgow to found the London Mechanics' Institution, the forerunner of the present-day Birkbeck College, a major center of modern continuing education. (Ashby, 1958, pp. 51–52) The mechanics' institutes spread into a genuine large-scale educational movement, but they were only marginally rooted in the British educational system. Even though they laid the foundation of a small set of institutions that grew in time from technical to technological, from institutes to colleges and universities, "in their own generation they did not bring technology within the pale of the formal educational system." (p. 53)

The new "anti-toga" Andersonian Institution, established in 1796 with only meager private funds, took up residence in the center of Glasgow, Scotland's industrial powerhouse, there to be closely tuned to technical training for the emerging industries of the day, notably textiles, ship-building and related metalwork on the shores of the river Clyde, and, naturally, some "brewing and distilling." (Butt, 1996, p. 46) Throughout the nineteenth century, under several changes in name and certain areas of training that need not detain us here, the Andersonian institutionalized a vocational character. By 1900 it was fixed on the vocational-technical path that only a few institutions in officially recognized UK higher education have trodden.

A classification offered by Ashby helps to highlight the peculiar place developed by the more technically minded UK institutions in the nineteenth and twentieth century. In his classic study of the impact of the scientific revolution on British universities, Ashby identified four main types of traditional European universities: the center of research-based scholarship and learning, typified by Berlin; the trainer of the learned professions, as in the age-old Bologna model; the "nursery of gentlemen, statesmen and administrators," as exemplified by Oxford and Cambridge; and "the staff college for technological specialists," as in Zurich. (Ashby, 1958; quoted in Sanderson, 1975, pp. 22–23) The antecedent units of today's University of Strathclyde developed slowly in the nineteenth century as *the* Scottish exemplar of the technological type, a place in northern Britain similar to the institutions that developed into the modern London Imperial College of Science and Technology in the south and the Manchester Institute of Science and Technology in the northwest of

England. As a supplier of technologists, the Glasgow Technical College made major strides as a place of "useful learning," and became known in the late nineteenth century not only for its direct connection to industry and commerce but also, with empire-serving graduates off to India and Africa, for its contribution to governmental imperial interests. The latter connection brought, in 1912, the designation "Royal" to the college; granted by George V after a trip to India that left him, as the story goes, "impressed with the quality and incidence of men from the Glasgow Technical College working on the Indian railways and waterworks. . . " (Sanderson, 1975, p. 14; Butt, 1996, p. 105)

The curriculum at the College was extremely technical at the turn of the century. Its nine departments of study consisted of civil, mechanical, electrical, chemical, and mining engineering, joined by agriculture, architecture, naval architecture, and metallurgy. (Butt, 1996, p. 105) New fields introduced in the early twentieth century had similar pragmatic pertinence: for example, bacteriology, to help industries in food-processing and brewing and governmental agencies in water supply and sewage; and pharmacy, "a subject requested by the Glasgow and West of Scotland Chemists' Association." (Butt, 1996, pp 106–107) All these practical academic fields had a growing interest in research, one encouraged in Britain by the increasingly obvious progress the Germans, the French, and the Americans were making in national research capability that seemingly spurred their economic development. The research interest gradually led to a stronger staff in such basic disciplines as chemistry, physics, and mathematics. Here, the technological subjects came first; the basic scientific fields followed.

The broader base was belatedly recognized by the UK national system when, in 1956, the Royal Technical College was redesignated the Royal College of Science and Technology, a title that lasted just a few years; in 1964 the "raising" of the college to university status, the present-day University of Strathclyde, was accomplished. By that time the Royal College could point out that it "produced more than ten percent of all those with university-level technology qualifications in Britain and more than all four of the Scottish Universities combined." (Butt, 1996, p. 164) The initial mechanics' institute, conceived by an odd professor in Glasgow, had become a major player in the small niche of UK technological institutions. Its substantial Scottish and national contribution won the day with the University Grants Committee (UGC) and the famous Robbins Committee of the early 1960s to gain university status.

But in the club of UK universities, ancient and modern, some sat at the head of the table and some sat well down past the salt. Industry and government might like technological institutions, but dons raised in the Oxford-Cambridge "nursery of gentlemen, statesmen and administrators" – Ashby's basic UK type – found such institutions wide of the mark. Writing during the 1958–1966 period, precisely when Strathclyde took up university status (Ashby, 1958, p. 66), sharply noted that it was difficult enough for British universities to adapt themselves to scientific thought [the defining British academic ideologue, Cardinal Newman, had thought research should be done elsewhere]; it is proving much more difficult for them to adapt themselves to technological thought. . . the crude engineer, the mere technologist (the very adjectives are symptoms of the attitude) are tolerated in universities because the state and industry are willing to finance them. Tolerated, but not assimilated: for the traditional don is not yet willing to admit that technologists may have anything intrinsic to contribute to academic life. It is not yet taken for granted that a faculty of technology enriches a university intellectually as well as materially.

Thus the technology pathway, from mechanics' institute to university, had major advantages and substantial disadvantages. It gave Strathclyde a distinctive place, as *the* Scottish institution, in a small subsector of British higher education. But it cast the institution in a mold that lacked status among British universities generally. It lacked humanities and could not claim the graces of "liberal education." It did not devote itself to basic research and thereby claim the warrant of "knowledge for its own sake." Instead, it was utilitarian, almost stubbornly so. When offered the option to move out of the center of Glasgow, where slums were encroaching, the new university of the early 1960s even refused the opportunity to become a "green-fields" university, an apparent advantage then being seized by a whole set of new institutions, from Sussex to Warwick, Essex to York. "Useful learning" was seen as best done in a "city-center" university, with commuting students, even part-time students if need be, and in whatever collection of city buildings, old and new, that could be linked to one huge edifice, the physical centerpiece of the Royal College, in existence since the 1910s.

During the 1960s and 1970s, Strathclyde went through its growing pains as a newly born technological university. While the institution was still a Royal College, Samuel C. Curran came on board as principal (1959) and stayed on for a long stay (1964–1980) as the first head of the new university. An outstanding nuclear physicist, very involved in wartime and postwar work in nuclear physics both in Britain and the United States, he led the fight for university status. When that status was achieved, a nearby Scottish College of Commerce was absorbed into the university. Diversification took place in business studies and modern languages; some diffusion into the humanities and social sciences was initiated, opening the door to economics, psychology, politics, administration, and history. (Butt, 1996, p. 166) Across the amalgamated parts, student enrollment totaled between 3,000 and 4,000 at the outset of the institution's life as a recognized university, a sizable total in a country where the historic commitment to small-scale universities led reformers of the 1960s to plan new universities for 2,000 to 4,000 students.

The 1960s and early 1970s were a period of optimistic growth in British higher education. Although staff at Strathclyde had good reason to feel underfunded by the UGC, receiving less than the sums awarded to the new "green-fields" universities then starting up, resources in all the technological fields were greatly expanded. Between 1960 and 1980, annual revenue for the university increased from 1 million to over 20 million pounds, capital assets from 2.6 million to 34 million. Land area was greatly increased from a mere 45 acres to 400 acres, student residential places from 40 to over 1,200. Income from research contracts that had barely existed at 24,000 pounds became a significant annual item of 3 million. (Butt, 1996, p. 194) All the traditional engineering fields added faculty, whether in mechanical or civil or electrical, or even mining, and such new hybrids were developed as bioengineering, a field that spanned the interface between life and physical sciences, medicine, and engineering. Later, in this expanding hybrid, Strathclyde developed a highly rated postgraduate department with extensive international reach and strong hospital and business linkages in artificial-organ development, a field with unlimited application.

Because the university was anxious to develop into a more comprehensive form, covering subjects not generally conceived as science and technology, about two-fifths of the students gradually appeared in the two areas of business studies and arts and social studies. (Butt, 1996, p. 189) The School of Business became very active, developing MBA and executive training programs out of which came the Graduate Business School that could function separately from the business courses offered for undergraduates. This would prove to be a major organizational reach out toward industry and will be discussed later as part of the institution's developmental periphery in the 1980s and 1990s. Another development, also initiated in the 1970s, significantly affected the character of Strathclyde in its later more entrepreneurial years: research in pharmaceutical chemistry directed by Professor John Stenlake led to a highly successful muscle relaxant, Atracurium which, when patented by the university and carried to market by the Wellcome pharmaceutical firm, turned out to be a lucrative source of income not only for the inventor and his research group but for the entire university as well. With Atracurium, the university discovered that royalty income could be a worthwhile income stream.

Strathclyde in the late 1970s was both old and young: old because Scottish and Glaswegian lineage was traceable back to 1796, young because its university status was achieved a mere decade and a half earlier. The old standing provided hoary tradition and deep roots in Scottish education, the new dignified the institution as Scotland's fifth university but presented it with the challenge, against well-established markers, of so much yet to be achieved. Would Strathclyde ever rank with Edinburgh (1583), Glasgow (1451), St. Andrews (1411), and Aberdeen (1495), the four august Scottish universities that had been so time-honored? Would it be on a plane with London and Manchester as a center of high science and technology? If the United Kingdom should self-consciously develop the "league tables" – the American style university rankings – that appeared only a decade later, where would Strathclyde appear? Probably in the lower half, because the national peer-review-and-assessment panels would be stocked with academics drawn from traditional disciplines not particularly enamored with useful knowledge. And when the most practical gauntlet of all was thrown down – budget cuts by the national government – what should Strathclyde do when its main patron declared it had run out of funds and would expect for untold years to come to exact "efficiency gains," a political euphemism for lowering unit-cost support? Would this mean increasing student-faculty ratios, more work for less money, less research support, and a fixed place in a second or third tier?

As observed in Warwick's case, the whole British system of higher education came under major budget cuts in the early 1980s at the hands of the Conservative (Thatcher) government that took power in 1979. Reductions had already been exacted in the 1970s by the prior Labor government: for example, funds would no longer be awarded to universities for their numerous foreign students, who then would have to pay their own full-cost fees. Now, after 1980, cuts were to be increased substantially, starting with a global reduction of some 17 percent, a sum that could, and was, apportioned by the UGC quite unevenly among the universities. What, then, should this oddly shaped new university do in a situation where the overall institutional ground was shifting radically? The Strathclyde response was broad and deep and relatively rapid. Between 1980 and 1995 the institution basically transformed itself, becoming in the process a leading case – arguably *the* leading case among Scottish universities – of a self-regulative university. As at Warwick and Twente, a complicated institutional story organizes well around the five elements that stand out as common features of transformation.

The 1980–1995 Transformation

Pride of place among the transforming elements goes to a *strengthened administrative core*. The first significant move made by Strathclyde in 1980–1981 was to bring on board a strong-minded vice-chancellor who set to work with considerable vigor to change the way the university made decisions. Graham Hills, a graduate of Birkbeck, had been a lecturer in chemistry at Imperial College, London, who then spent 18 years (1962–1980) as professor and administrator at Southampton University, serving as dean of science and deputy vice-chancellor. (Butts, 1996, p. 196) There he worked both on university-industry relations, particularly on the utility of research institutes that would bridge this divide, and on the possibility of greater control in financial matters that could be occasioned by budgetary devolution. How to bridge to industry and how to manage financial devolution were key concerns of the new campus head, problems considerably intensified by the external threat of severe governmental cuts.

Hills set to work to bring about some drastic organizational changes that would help, indeed force, the university to improve the way that it "allocates and re-allocates its resources." (Hills, 1981) Assuming that decisions in universities are best made at local levels, the concept of budgeting devolution was pushed. But devolution to what units? Academic groupings larger than departments were deemed necessary, even units larger than the nine schools into which the departments were then organized. An early step then was to consolidate both departments and schools into four major faculties of science, engineering, business, and arts and social sciences, and then to begin to devolve the budget to these four units, each to be headed by a strengthened dean. A second major step that took some years to work out was then to find centralizing devices that would hold the four main sectors together. Here, changes in budget and organization had to go hand in hand. The budgetary device was to retain part of the money from the four faculties: in the name of overall institutional interest, a "strategic fund" would be held by the center. But what should be the nature of the center that would look after the institutional interest? A crucial question everywhere.

As at most other UK universities at the time, the historic center at Strathclyde was quite soft; overall direction was diffused in a rabbit warren of committees that proliferated over time as offsprings of senate, court, and the principal's office. The university historian, John Butt, reported (in interview) that over 50 central committees were then responsible for the overall institutional interest. With this diffusion, there was a certain lassitude of purpose. Nearest to a focal point was an academic planning committee of about 20 members, responsible to senate, consisting largely of elected senate members and nine deans. It took virtually a decade of incremental changes to radically reduce the role of the traditional committee system and to replace it with a structure that retained the usual reactive roles of court and senate as the two top formally responsible units, but also gave the center a proactive managerial peak, a focal point that at the outset could be likened to a cabinet or a committee of committees. A first step was to reduce the size of the ungainly academic planning committee: participating deans were cut from nine to four, senate representation could also logically be reduced, and one or two lay members of court could also be in attendance. A second step was to reform this committee as the Joint Policy Committee (JPC), with members from the administration, senate, and court. JPC ran into much difficulty: faculty and administrators remembered a decade later, in 1996 interviews, that its deliberations were routinely stalled by "warriors" who were liberally prepared to veto disagreeable issues. Something else had to be ventured.

The something else was spurred by a national report on the (in)efficiency of British universities. The 1985 *Report of the Steering Committee for Efficiency Studies in Universities*, commissioned by the national Committee of Vice-Chancellors and Principals (CVCP) and known as the Jarrett Report, hit hard at the apparent sluggishness of British universities: they lacked "a clear view of what they wanted to do," and, typically, they did not have "the necessary structure to effect adequate rates of change and the will to produce it. We see this as the greatest need for the universities in their preparation for the period up to the end of this century." (Committee of Vice-Chancellors and Principals (CVCP) 1985, p. 12) According to the report, hard times were now upon the universities; they would have to choose among their departments and activities even though they lacked the organized means of doing so. The Jarrett Report made ten recommendations to the universities. It stressed that the vice chancellor (or principal) had to be recognized "not only as academic leader but also as chief executive"; that budgets needed to be delegated to appropriate subcenters, which were then held responsible for their achievements; that there should be fewer committees involving fewer people and more delegated activity to "officers of the university"; and, important, that there ought to be a central "planning and resources committee of strictly limited size. . . with the Vice-Chancellor as Chairman," a particular place where a university could "bring planning, resource allocation, and accountability together into one corporate process linking academic, financial, and physical aspects." (p. 36)

The Jarrett Report was not much liked by British academics: industrialists were heavily involved and businesslike corporate models much touted. For many it smacked of "hard managerialism." But Strathclyde took the report very seriously. It established its own Committee on the Organisation and Effectiveness of Decision-Making whose members stated, in a 1986 report, that the traditional approach to university decision making "presented formidable obstacles to change"; and that "'hard times' demand 'hard choices' which would require a more focused administration." (p. 3) The report saw the university's Joint Policy Committee as "both unsatisfactory and too large," and recommended that it be replaced by a leaner "Committee of Management."

That successor committee, born in 1987 as the University Management Group (UMG), became the lasting centerpiece of a strengthened administrative core. UMG was established not as an instrument of either court or senate, but as an independent entity composed of members who officially were not drawn from either of the two much larger overarching bodies. As put at the university: "It reports to court and senate but is not a creature of either." UMG became constituted in time by five deans, coming "up" or "to" the center from the main faculty units, and about an equal number of senior central officers: principal, a vice-principal, a vice-principal elect, a deputy principal, and the university secretary. Important, all the deans are elected to their deanships by academics within their individual faculties and several of the central officers are also elected to short-term posts. The faculty is then very involved in deciding who may join the central management group. Only the secretary, head of administration, is a true manager in the normal use of the term. But UMG could invite other administrators, such as the director of finance, to sit in on its biweekly meetings. As it worked out over time, UMG also became supported by the UMG Secretariat that met weekly, reviewed the upcoming agenda, and prepared a paper, circulated before the next UMG meeting, that earmarked some items to be taken as read and other to be set aside for discussion. The secretariat serves as gate-keeper of the in-and-out flow of UMG papers. By the mid-1990s the UMG operation had become "all very business-like"; it "runs a tight schedule." To help insure transparency, UMG even institutionalized a full-time secretary responsible for getting reports out promptly in three directions: to court, to senate, and to the university newsletter, a public document made available to staff, students, and the outside world.

The university administration was strengthened by uniting it under one head, the university secretary; at the end of the 1980s, the former two top administrative positions, bursar and registrar, were eliminated. Occupying the pivotal post of secretary since its establishment, Peter West has made a point of hiring able senior administrators, often drawn from outside the university ranks, to run the growing major administrative areas, to serve in the UMG Secretariat, and to act as representatives of the center in approving actions generated in departments and faculties.

Administrators and faculty alike in the mid-1990s pointed to the UMG as the embodiment of the difference between this institution and other universities in Scotland, perhaps from nearly all others in the UK: "UMG is the key here"; "UMG is one thing that makes Strathclyde unique." As an institutional core worked out over years of struggle and adjustment, it has been viewed within the institution as a particularly effective response to the Jarrett Report and to other critical perceptions of university ineptitude. It was "the most dramatic [response] of any I know"; it represented a move to "a private sector model of management"; it reduced "rule by faculty committees." The academic senate became recognized as strong on discussion of issues but weak on action. As the central component of a strengthened administrative core, one that had assumed much operational authority, UMG became the action group that could "get-up-and-go."

Critical in understanding the importance of the Strathclyde UMG is the crucial role it has played in airing and then smoothing over the conflict between new managerial values and traditional academic ones. UMG is not a body of central administrators, grouped around a CEO (chief executive officer): most of its members are from the faculty. Elected deans play a central role: they come to the UMG as representatives of their university sectors; they then find they must also consider the overall institutional interest. The UMG has been able to set a teamwork-oriented tone: there is no place for the partisan warrior, the representative pushing his or her own group interest at all cost. "Obviously" destructive, the latter posture pushes the institution toward a Hobbsian war of all against all. Deans can and do assert the individual interests of their faculties, but they must also go beyond them if they are not to be personally embarrassed. Their ongoing intense interaction on the UMG, where they are members as major "budget-holders," presses them to assume responsibility for the entire university. Their lot is to work together with the equal number of central officials grouped around the principal who are also significant budget-holders. Hence, the deans at Strathclyde (five in the mid-1990s) may be seen as classic cases of organizational middlemen; their roles put them squarely in a position where, as the price of effectiveness, two broad sets of values must be reconciled. In the UMG framework they must handle, issue by issue, the clash between managerial and academic values and the opposition between the interests of the center and the interests of the parts. In reconciling values and interests, the UMG has become a much-needed smoothing mechanism.

A change of principals in 1990 also moved direction at the top from a posture of strong, personal leadership to a more collective, collegial form. Graham Hills felt obliged to push hard at the faculty throughout his term. Contentiousness in senate meetings and in the early new central bodies that led to the formation of the UMG came from both sides. Hills, later Sir Graham, also worked hard to build the university a decent physical plant, maintaining that in the early 1980s, Strathclyde was "the ugliest university" in the UK. Office and classroom buildings were constructed and refurbished; student residencies were improved and turned into a "student village"; landscaping gave touches of greenery to the pathways of a rocky hillside location. Work on the physical plant required new imaginative forms of capital finance in lieu of a fast-disappearing government subsidy. This brought more corporate-type managerialism that again pushed hard at softer academic norms. Busy with many outside obligations, Hills left the university after nearly a decade in office in which much had been accomplished.

The new "V-C," John Arbuthnott, a microbiologist, had the temperament to work as a first-among-equals in the collective leadership of the UMG and related central bodies. Under his leadership the UMG developed easier collegial relationships that helped smooth the way among the always contentious issues of day-to-day administration and long-term directions of effort. A leading scientist at the university, looking back from the vantage point of the mid-1990s said, "Sir Graham was right on a lot of things. . . We had almost got to sleep in the early 80s. . . For his first five years he was the right man, especially when he made all these structural changes. . . Then he became very involved externally, and lost his internal contacts." Now, in the mid-1990s, the scientist went on, we have "soft management," with very good central administrators interacting with the five deans on the UMG. "The UMG is doing a good job at processing the business. . . It is doing as well as it could on synthesizing the academic business. . . The job of the principal now is to check on the faculties. . . The dynamics of trust between the academics and the administrative community is so important." Another significant, experienced figure at the university, speaking of "the saga of the principals," stated: Hills was a "completely fresh wind of change. . . he brought everything up [as a university] and built up a perception." Arbuthnott has "made it a reality. . . He has done that, and done it beautifully." The critical item in the UMG is "that at the end of the day the five deans are pulling in the same direction." And, in the opinion of a third respondent who observed the need for strong collegiality in university management, "for something to succeed in a university, many people have to be willing to make it happen."

Strathclyde has also learned to make good use of respected and supportive nonacademics by having two senior "lay" members of court regularly attend UMG meetings. The Jarrett Report of the mid-1980s had called for the universities to make better use of their lay members. Strathclyde felt in the mid-1990s that it had successfully done this, arguably more than any other British university, by so clearly including two members of court in the peak managerial group. A central administrator noted: "their influence is profound," that "their presence and influence has helped to draw UMG away from an academic mode of discussion towards a managerial one."

Just as Strathclyde worked out an appreciably strengthened administrative core to provide a steering capacity, it was also busy during the 1980s and early 1990s in fashioning a major *developmental periphery*. Outreach took three forms: new administrative offices; outwardly oriented research centers; and teaching units that served nontraditional segments of the population.

A highly effective administrative unit that soon operated under the title of "Research and Development Services" greatly expanded the connection of the university to outside groups. Hills hired in the early 1980s Hugh Thomson, an electrical engineer who had become expert in the management of spin-off and start-up companies, to promote "technology transfer" at Strathclyde. His office started out in 1984 with just two professionals: Thomson himself and a financial research-contract officer drawn from the existing administration. A first highly proactive step was to find out what was going on in Brussels, the headquarters of the European Commission (EC). A consultant hired for this purpose came home with the news that the EC could supply more than 60 funding opportunities for the university. Immediately hired as a full-timer dedicated to the EC relationship, apparently the first in UK universities, the new staff member helped raise 900,000 pounds the first year. The oversight faculty committee then decided that his one-year contract could be lengthened! A second person, later hired, gave Strathclyde a two-person staff dedicated to working the hallways of the Brussels bureaucracy, to find possible funding sources for projects, and to translate Eurocratese into understandable prose for faculty and administrators back home.

The EC experience indicated that this R&D office could be more than a place for tracking contracts. It could emulate an aggressive business that took risks on short-term investments possibly leading to major long-term returns. In the mid-1980s, to make money from patents, the office moved systematically into "intellectual property." Strathclyde was already receiving about one million pounds a year from Atracurium, the drug synthesized by Professor Stenlake and jointly patented by him and the university. Hiring an exceedingly dynamic "intellectual property officer" (again, apparently the first fulltime staff in the UK academic world), the university set to work to construct gradually a portfolio of patents that might – or might not – become commercially viable;

it was fully aware that many inventions could take years to generate income and that "hits" are greatly outnumbered by "misses." Gradually an engineering sector developed in this portfolio which listed possible industrial partners located in Scotland and the UK. But most important, a health-care grouping came on strong. It partnerships were truly international and were built on a network of ties to developing countries. Here the office became in effect an entrepreneurial and managerial arm of the Strathclyde Institute for Drug Research (SIDR) described later in this chapter.

When another contract manager was hired about the same time, particularly to negotiate better deals on research contracts, the office had a critical mass of five professionals. By the mid-1990s it had grown from its original two to 12 officers, all more than paying their way, covering the European Union possibilities, intellectual property, contracts, research marketing, and the formation of new institutes and companies. In Scotland, only the University of Edinburgh had a larger staff for such purposes; there a major medical school was involved. In the UK at large, Strathclyde in the mid-1990s was one of a small minority of universities having such a sizable R&D outreach office. Across a decade of development that office has also won status and authority in the university. Its relationships with academic staff have been construed as voluntary by them. Yet its voice has risen to the point where the director, now representing the institutional interest, signs off on proposals heading toward outside support. Here, "vetoes" have been minimized by helping academic staff from the beginning to start proposals and improve them before submission. The office became a good case of an organizational unit, born in the developmental periphery, gradually moving from a marginal status to fuse with academic faculties and departments as well as established units of central administration.

The Research and Consultancy Services office (mid-1990s title), has also promoted an incubator unit on campus. Here small firms started from within or outside the university can benefit from initial location in a university setting and can incubate for three to four years before being pushed out (by annually rising rents!) into the cruel world, perhaps to the West of Scotland Science Park, shared with the University of Glasgow, 20 minutes away. This park contains research offices of industrial firms as well as new university spin-offs. Projected changes in the mid-1990s included the development of a new park near Strathclyde, supported by the city of Glasgow, and a shift from "low-tech" to "high-tech" in firm composition. Along the lines of science park management, the university found much to admire at Heriot-Watt, a Scottish university located in Edinburgh. For a university science park to be highly successful, the Strathclyde office came to feel that half-hearted measures will not do: "You have to work at it!"; "You have to manage it!" The Heriot-Watt park was seen as the most successful one in Scotland because it was led by "can do" people who had vigorously managed it. Tentative planning at Strathclyde in the mid-1990s was pointed to go and do the same.

The second major component of Strathclyde's new developmental periphery consisted of a growing number of interdisciplinary research centers so outward-oriented that they even accepted "a market-pull component to their research planning." (University of Strathclyde, early 1990s, p. 3) Looking for "technology transfer highways," the university first sought to promote research units *in* departments, and then moved on to "more autonomous research institutes" that in many cases could fashion "collaborative, joint venture, and other partnership relationships with industry." Venturing further, they would also pay attention to the policies of government departments, development agencies, and research funding circles. (pp. 4–5) During this process, the university wanted to work out "the steady state requirements" of dynamic research groups, and in the mid-1990s, it could point to over 20 research institutes, not counting ones in germination. These centers varied in substantive content. The Fraser of Allander Institute, largely based in the social sciences, and dating from 1975, is a leading research and forecasting unit on the state of the Scottish economy. The European Policies Research Centre, also long established, does detailed policy research for government departments and international organizations, especially on regional development within the EU. Institutes in the science and engineering fields deal with advanced structural materials, information technology, electrical power engineering, network management in communication systems, and smart structures technology. (pp. 6–16)

A particularly dynamic and successful instance of research center outreach is Strathclyde's Institute for Drug Research (SIDR), underway since 1988 within the faculty of science. Pharmaceuticals, from the beginning, were a promising area. Experience with Atracurium, a drug that generated income from 1986 on and significant sums several years later, dramatized for all to see that this sector was worthy of further exploration. Professor Peter Waterman in pharmaceutical sciences had pursued the extraction of potentially useful products from natural plant materials for many years. The new institute was set up to focus on the generation of both chemical and natural products. Instead of "blue-sky research," it aimed to do applied research with a clear agenda of generating intellectual property licensable to industry.

With a full-time research staff of 20 and over 50 faculty members participating from five departments, the institute could claim in the mid-1990s over four million dollars per year of royalty income from drug-related work. It had generated over 50 contracts, mainly from industry, totaling over seven million dollars in research support, and was involved in a steady stream of patent applications and licensing opportunities. Estimating downstream hits and misses (Strathclyde had experienced the latter), the responsible intellectual property officer in Research and Consultory Services was willing in 1996 to publicly claim the "potential value of portfolio" in this area to be 28 million dollars annually.

Beyond investing in chemically synthesized compounds such as Atracurium, SIDR has systematically pursued the production of natural health products that offer licensing opportunities: antidepressants, antiobesity compounds, and antifungal compounds. Following up on Professor Waterman's long engagement in developing societies, SIDR and Research & Consultancy Services together worked out an international network – a "natural product network" – with partner suppliers in countries in Africa, South America, Asia, Australia, and even Europe (Spain). The partner research centers supply leaves, bark, seeds, the upper parts of plants, not roots, an environmentally sustainable way of providing plant materials. Through "acquisition agreements" that give 60 percent of related income to the home country, Strathclyde developed worldwide access to a "library of plants." The materials examined at the SIDR could also be sold to others to analyze: "selling agreements" became especially numerous with Japanese pharmaceutical houses.

The senior intellectual-property officer has not only traveled widely to developing societies to scout and identify possible acquisitions but also has gone to biotechnical firms in Japan and the United States (for example to California, Massachusetts, and New Jersey) to sell products. In this effort Strathclyde is not hesitant; confident that it has a sustainable form of organization, based on trust and respect worked out over a number of years – nothing "hit-and-miss" – and certain that its competition is weak – it is difficult for other universities and especially industrial firms to replicate its operation – its possibilities are endless. Strathclyde is well-placed to interface with science in developing societies. The bilateral agreements on plant-material acquisition not only give specific research centers in those societies some sustainable income but also offer scientists in those centers a potentially visible and viable niche in the fast-moving international science base. (University of Strathclyde, 1996b)

This fascinating long-term line of research development was one on which some central figures at the university felt it "could hang its hat." There was reason for optimism, especially if an always changing, more effective organization could be devised to expand research and development *and* recover income. At an international conference in eastern Europe, halfway through 1996, the secretary of the university, Peter West, announced that following upon the success of SIDR, "a commercial company, to be known as Drug Discovery Research Ltd is about to be launched: its Business Plan estimates annual royalty income of at least £60M by year 20." (West, 1996b, p. 5) Here was a Strathclyde niche, one worthy of further investment and sustained exploratory development. The niche was squarely in the realm of knowledge transfer: bringing knowledge "to the market, through company formation, licensing, and the general exploitation of the university's intellectual property." The end result would be improved economic performance. With royalty income already about four million pounds each year, Strathclyde could see itself (on this feature) among the top ten universities in the world and "the most successful university in Europe." (West, 1996a, p. 130)

Beyond establishing boundary-spanning new development offices and research centers, Strathclyde has also widely extended its teaching outreach. A self-financing Graduate Business School, the campus's second business school, could claim the awarding in the 1990s of more MBAs than the rest of Scotland combined, *and* a line of work that through its many programs produced substantial income. "Foreign earnings, especially from the MBA distance learning courses, led to the Queen's Award for Export Achievement in 1993, the Graduate Business School being the only educational institution to win the award up to that time." (Butt, 1996, p. 238) When the university agreed in the early 1990s to a merger with the Jordanhill College of Education, also located in Glasgow, and then organized the acquired staff as a fifth faculty, it added in one blow 2,500 students and an array of university-school connections and related specific programs. (Arbuthnott and Bone, 1993) Both sides benefited. Jordanhill, which brought no competing courses and no overlapping staff, needed a university home for its teacher training to keep up with the times. From the university view: "Although Strathclyde was well over 8,000 students, it had a surprisingly small number of faculties, and could obviously benefit from taking on an additional role as provider of the training to a large proportion of Scotland's teachers." (p. 109) This is not exactly the way most universities think of teacher training! Strathclyde's orientation to "useful learning" helped to give a favorable cast to the hard work of melding the culture of a large, traditional teachers college with the research-centered culture of an ambitious university. The university was realistic: "A successful merger may take as long as ten years to become a reality." (p. 118) Aside from first and higher degrees, "diploma" awards at the university then jumped fourfold; from somewhat over 400 a year in 1990–1991 to over 1600 in 1995–1996. Jordanhill became a second campus in a suburban location, and the university became a place that trained more school teachers than any other institution in the UK.

Bioengineering, a small highly specialized graduate program focused on developing artificial organs, is a third illuminating instance of teaching outreach. Here research and instruction involve links to hospitals and industry. Students return to the university from exterior practice, outside experts teach as "honorary" faculty, and cooperative ties and distance-learning courses develop internationally, from Eastern Europe to Japan. With senior professors serving as organizers and continuing officers of the International Society for Artificial Organs, in which Japanese and American membership is large, the university's small bioengineering program became a "high profile unit." Its research program has earned a "5," the top score, in the 1988 and 1992 rounds of UK research ratings; its teaching program, consisting of short courses presented at the university and abroad, carries out face-to-face instruction on an international basis. (Barbanel, 1993; Paul, 1993; Courtney, 1993) Here indeed is a university unit characterized by "pragmatic pertinence"; its teaching and learning is thoroughly fused with research at the same time that outreach is promoted vigorously and effectively.

The extensive developmental periphery, as we saw at Warwick and Twente, exists only in part as a separate element at Strathclyde. It overlaps with *the stimulated academic heartland*, our element for referencing core academic faculties and departments. Outreaching research centers fall under different faculties; for example, the Institute for Drug Research, located formally in the Faculty of Science, draws faculty to it, especially in leadership roles, from many departments. The university's self-financing second business school is governed for academic purposes by the dean and the Faculty of Business, and is thereby linked to what goes on in the first business school. The Jordanhill College of Education, gradually absorbed operationally as a Faculty of Education, is thereby formally located as one of the five faculties that constitute the meso-mainline infrastructure of the university. The Bioengineering Unit straddles the periphery-core line. Thus, even though units play such an important role in outreach that we can appropriately portray them as part of a developmental periphery, we need also to recognize that they are situated close to the academic heartland. Such integration, of course, is much to be desired.

A leading case of a true heartland department at Strathclyde is the Department of Electronic and Electrical Engineering (EEE), located within the Faculty of Engineering. From its central interior perch it has steadily developed its own entrepreneurship and outreach. The largest department in the largest faculty, it has about 50 academics distributed in five internal research groups. The department feels it is "a steeple" unit, doing well in national assessments of teaching and research, and, in its field, compared with the best institutions in the UK, such as Southampton, Imperial College, University College London, and the University of Edinburgh. It can claim "close and successful collaboration with industrial and academic bodies within and outside the UK," to the tune of over 200 firms and over 50 universities that range as far afield as the United States and China. (University of Strathclyde, 1994, pp. 36–38) Its research monies in the mid-1990s came about equally from the British government, the European Union, and industry.

Department organization is important in serving various functions, reaching in different directions, and remaining flexible. EEE sees the department as a whole as the unit responsible for undergraduate teaching. The five research divisions, focused on departmental subareas, promote research activity and train advanced students. These second level units can be given budgetary lump sums and allowed to operate quite autonomously: they select projects according to their disciplinary special interests. At a third level, staff members can make their own linkages to industrial firms, government departments, and other external bodies. Flexibility is achieved at the second and third levels and then percolates upward to the higher departmental plane; for example, to change course materials for undergraduates. The EEE is an excellent example of modern departmental organization that enables a close integration of research, teaching, and study. (Clark, 1995) All staff members are encouraged to do research.

The university has filed over a dozen patents from work in this department, some jointly with industrial firms. The department's discretionary monies raised primarily from research contracts with industry and the European Union may be split as many as five ways, with shares going to the investigator, his or her research division, the department, the faculty, and the university as a whole. Top-slicing at Strathclyde is a contentious art, but everyone gets something from the results of the entrepreneurial actions of seeking outside funding. The department is also involved in a new five-year study program of "entrepreneurship for students" that has been worked out between the two faculties of engineering and business.

Before leaving EEE we can touch briefly on the focus of the Smart Structures Research Institute, started in 1991 by the Optoelectronics Division of the department, which quickly developed multiple links with other departments and faculties. What is a smart structure? A definition will help (University of Strathclyde, 1994, p. 106):

> A smart structure is one which is capable of responding to its environment, for example, by modifying its stiffness, colour, shape, thermal conductivity, or position depending upon external parameters. Smart structures involve intimately embedded sensors to monitor these external parameters, adaptive intelligence to interpret the data from the sensor array and embedded activators which, through the necessary control system, provide the appropriate structural response.

Possible applications for such structures range through civil, aerospace, and automotive engineering, and beyond. It is an "exciting possibility" and "an intriguing prospect" that "the sensory system, the processing and the actuation can all be available within an intelligent material. . ." (p. 106) The institute is invested in basic research, collaborative research with industry, and dissemination: its membership program has entailed international seminars in Glasgow, London, and Paris, with significant representation from Japan and the United States. As of 1994, the institute felt it was "unique in Europe and has already raised the profile of Strathclyde over a very broad spectrum of industries and government agencies." (p. 106)

Can reasoning by analogy from physical structures to social structures offer an idea or two suggestive of adaptive university organization? Can "intimately embedded sensors" warn when a university is growing too rigid or too incongruent with its environment? Can a monitoring office be capable of intelligent interpretation of received signals? Most intriguing of all, could "embedded actuators. . . through the necessary control system, provide the appropriate structural response?" Outreach offices in a university's developmental periphery clearly can serve as embedded sensors; a strengthened administration core can serve as a monitor and an embedded actuator with the power to make structural responses. An entrepreneurial attitude spread throughout the academic heartland can be seen as a buildup of many embedded sensors, monitors, and actuators. Following this analogy, the pathways of entrepreneurial development are means of constructing smart universities more capable than dull counterparts of adaptive behavior.

Turning to the social sciences and humanities, it is much more difficult for these fields to fashion links to industry and other external sectors. But the entrepreneurial attitude is also clearly evident in Strathclyde's Faculty of Arts and Social Sciences. The smallest of the faculties, it operates with six small departments, some multidisciplinary, and ten subject areas. Five departments have internal research centers and the number of "research students" is growing. The faculty works with local government and has an esteemed Centre for the Study of Public Policy directed by Richard Rose. Since governmental cuts are predicted to continue, faculty members feel compelled to "do things that bring in money" – a certain amount of "going with the market" of student demand and with the markets of outside organizational interests. They have diligently attempted therefore to attract more students through, for example, the development of Scottish studies, European studies, and women's studies. Part-time students have become more attractive. And since this faculty is relatively poor, and their funding is less diversified, it has to watch expenses very carefully. Low enrollment classes are cut, early retirements encouraged. The student-teacher ratio climbed in the mid-1990s to 18:1. Luckily, when the faculty has to "bid" for money from the university's central strategic fund, it has received more than its share, indicating that it has benefited from the cross-subsidization so many universities increasingly use to keep their poorer departments from sinking further into poverty. In this Faculty of Arts and Social Sciences any attempt to build in one area generally means taking faculty positions from another or replacing expensive senior faculty with less-costly junior faculty. Entrepreneurial life is here particularly difficult, but with the government reducing its support, there is no other answer for maintaining viable departments.

The efforts of Strathclyde's strengthened steering core, the extensive enlargement of its developmental periphery, and the spread of entrepreneurial attitudes and actions in the heartland departments all led toward *diversified income*. Strathclyde, like Warwick, responded relatively early and forcefully to the need to raise money from nongovernment sources and to learn to use discretionary money for self-regulation. Core government support for the university slipped from 75 percent of total income in 1970 to 64 percent in 1980 down to 48 percent in 1990 – and still further to 45 percent in 1995 (Table 4–1). With second-stream income from government research councils a relatively small item, university support has been augmented largely by third-stream income: what was a 14 percent contribution in 1970 became 31 percent in 1980 and 47 percent in 1990. Still rising, it reached over 50 percent in 1995. Intellectual property income has become a Strathclyde specialty. In 1994–1995, it was second among the over 100 UK universities on "income from intellectual property rights" (*The Times Higher Education Supplement* (*THES*), Nov. 1, 1996, p. 13). The University of Edinburgh, with a medical school, was first; Oxford and Cambridge did not appear in the top ten. Even Imperial College London had income from this source that was only one-seventh of Strathclyde's. Third-stream income has gone a long way to boost the scale and scope of Strathclyde's operation. Leaving aside medical-school components of the other Scottish universities, it had surpassed the University of Glasgow in income magnitude and ranked close to the largest one, the University of Edinburgh.

Third-stream income has helped Strathclyde to build reserves at both university and department levels; this adds flexibility in managing change. To build reserves, of course, a university must be able to carry over surpluses from one year to the next. Because any surplus appeared to be funding in advance, the UK Treasury insisted "it will not fund in advance of needs." Funding councils then lent support: they made the broad assumption that universities first use treasury monies and that surpluses are thereby generated out of nonpublic sources. Then the extra money does not belong to the government but to the university. And under decentralized budgeting, some share of a surplus becomes department reserves. The internal issue then is how much money departments retain to carry forward and how much is melded into a common university reserve. At Strathclyde in the mid-1990s, the balance had become heavily skewed toward the departments – ten million pounds in the departments, one and one-half million at the center – causing, in this always contentious matter, deep concern at the center over a drained "strategic fund." Dividing up surpluses itself becomes a strategic decision, and defines central as opposed to departmental steer.

Finally, *institutional beliefs* have played an important role in guiding and rationalizing change. The traditional idea of "useful learning" in itself has become a modern cohesive force at Strathclyde. A senior scientist pointed out in interview that useful learning had become a comfortable institutional idea. Everybody accepts it; everything works around it; an "ethos" permeating the

TABLE 4–1

Sources of Financial Support, University of Strathclyde 1970–1995
(millions of British pounds)

	Core Support		Research Councils		All Other Sources*		Total	
Year	Amount	Percent	Amount	Percent	Amount	Percent	Amount	Percent
1970	3.8	75	0.6	11	0.7	14	5.1	100
1975	8.3	80	1.0	10	1.1	10	10.4	100
1980	15.6	64	1.2	5	7.7	31	24.5	100
1985	24.9	59	2.0	5	14.9	36	41.8	100
1990	38.3	48	3.8	5	37.5	47	79.6	100
1995	59.8	45	5.8	4	67.1	51	132.7	100

*Includes tuition fees
Source: Trend data compiled by David Coyle, Finance Officer, University of Strathclyde

heartland defines the university as "a place of useful learning." There was little strain between views of what is "basic" and what is "applied." Under the banner of useful learning, the university could readily claim as part of its overall doctrine that it was engaged in "strategic research," a concept so much in vogue in the views of government and industry in the UK that it could be seen at Strathclyde as "a very useful political safety net." And as reported in interview, the idea of usefulness put the university more on a parallel with the way that people think of business: then the idea becomes an academic equivalent of a broad business-type mission. In contrast, the nearby much older and more diffuse University of Glasgow was seen as dependent on "ancient foundations" as the nearest thing to a cohesive force.

Usefulness was given particular point in a claim that the university was committed to "closing the gap between industry and universities." This was the central idea in "The Strathclyde Phenomenon," a statement offered by Graham Hills and Hugh Thomson at the beginning of the 1990s which claimed that beyond *The Cambridge Phenomenon* (the title of a book describing the success of the Cambridge Science Park), there was now to be found a Strathclyde idea of more broadly harnessing university knowledge "to the business of wealth creation," forging "sharply focused connections between the university's research strengths and the discerned interests of a particular company or business." (University of Strathclyde, early 1990s, p. 1) Beyond a science park, a whole university stood ready to be helpful. The "phenomenon" went beyond specific linking structures:

> it is mostly about attitudes. It is about the attitude of academic staff willing to engage in an additional stratum of research activity which imposes considerable business disciplines, requires multi-disciplinary teamwork across traditional department and faculty boundaries, and accepts a market-pull component to their research planning. It also is about the attitude of the university in being willing to support such initiatives and to invest in the management costs necessary to bring them about. (p. 3)

The ideas of useful learning, strategic research, and knowledge transfer, at Strathclyde, come to imply one another. They came together as a belief system that has become an all-university culture. They are expressed in outreach willingness on the part of faculty and entrepreneurial initiative on the part of central administration. They stress that a place of useful learning must be a "well-administered place." Finally, they include the claim that the faculty value flexibility and change. They are defined as always willing to explore "a range of possibilities" out of which adaptive responses can be made to new political initiatives and other changes in the environment. As put sharply in a statement by the Faculty of Science, the biggest risk that should be avoided at all costs is to passively stand in place: "To do nothing is the equivalent of allowing the commencement of 'death by 1000 cuts'." (University of Strathclyde, 1996c, p. 12)

Conclusion

Strathclyde University is an admirable third case for a study of entrepreneurial universities. Starting from a low, even marginal, status, it struggled mightily to blossom as a British university. As a technical college raised to university status, and thereby to become a new university of the mid-1960s, the institution was not built around a comprehensive array of departments in the arts and sciences, let alone physically located in green fields. Little had been done to make the institution even look like a British-style university. There was no way Strathclyde could clone the hoary and honorable traditions, very meaningful for the Scottish population, of the four ancient Scottish universities. The institution would have to elaborate a university self out of its technological base, its proven capacity ("core competence") in engineering and applied science.

The five common elements highlighted in this study were involved pathways of its transformation after 1980. A much strengthened administrative core became a decisive element. A new central body focused university-wide authority in a way not evident before. Contributing to its steering capacity was a more focused and better integrated small body of central administrators, now more professional and expert. Deanships of the four-turned-five faculties became highly significant posts, key rings in an institutional backbone, with budget decentralization pressuring faculties to develop themselves. Deans were also brought to the institutional center, as members of the UMG, there to play a second role as caretakers of broad institutional interests – another critical step. Led by the principal, "at the end of the day" the deans had to be pulling together if a transformed Strathclyde were to work.

A much enlarged developmental periphery, promoted by the administrative core, also came to play an essential role, giving Strathclyde new infrastructure for greatly extended outreach that would also explore and systematically tap new income streams. Highly imaginative steps in R&D outreach, worthy of note by other universities, led to the development of systematic ways to pursue the exploitation of "intellectual property." The outreach has steadily enabled Strathclyde to diversify its income, another critical element for creating an entrepreneurial edge. Income diversification increased local discretion – for faculties, departments, research centers, and individual faculty members as well as the central steering group. Third-stream incomes are helpful in the best of times. In the worst of times – the years since the early 1980s for governmental financing of British higher education – those incomes are critical to institutional health and progress. Strathclyde had, in its own estimation, particularly achieved "a balanced portfolio of research income streams."

Entrepreneurship at Strathclyde has increasingly not been left to a few segments of the campus but has spread across the faculties and departments that compose the academic heartland. They all have to become motivated to think about which steps will effect dependable relationships with outside groups, *and* which will adapt to changing student interests. Decisions have had to be made to select one program over another, one department over another, one new interdisciplinary field to be backed even as an older specialty is let go or allowed to slide to the margin. Self-financing avenues of program development have become increasingly attractive – the proliferation of MBA degree programs in the Faculty of Business is one example. Courses that will increase student enrollment and mainline income have been chosen.

Encouraging such actions, and providing rationalizations for them, has been a set of change-oriented ideas and beliefs that cluster under the broad banner of useful learning. Strathclyde has been blessed in this regard. An historic identity centered on practical usefulness and involvement with industry has resonated well with national demands for "university relevance," engagement in "strategic research," and "knowledge transfer." Strathclyde could claim that this had been its focus all along – witness the demonstrated and acclaimed usefulness for the Empire in the late nineteenth century – while the more traditional universities were otherwise preoccupied. It could claim the forward-looking attitudes of problem solving in engineering and applied science. As part of "the Strathclyde Phenomenon," the institution could hold up the belief that among the universities of Scotland it had demonstrated a particular capacity to meet industry halfway. If the "development gap" was even to be closed, the "Strathclyde way" would contribute essential bridging steps.

Strathclyde's 1980–1995 development left the institution all the more ambitious to be thought well of as a British university. Having started out near the bottom of the status ladder, its progress in academic research had led by the mid-1990s to the stated intention to climb in the next decade or so into the ranks of the top 20 UK universities. (University of Strathclyde, 1995, p. 1) This would be a tall order, especially since rankings and images formed around traditional basic research and brought to bear in national review panels did not favor "pragmatic pertinence." An official at Strathclyde noted in the early 1990s the sheer irony of research-rating exercises, in a nation desperately seeking university effort which would stimulate economic progress, that gave little credit for industry-relevance research and development and for self-generated income that kept research alive when otherwise it would have died. However difficult to achieve, a top 20 ambition pointed to a strengthened self-concept. It asserted that transformation at Strathclyde was a work in progress, with an up-market trajectory established by the hard work of the 1980s and early 1990s. By "targeted investment in a few key disciplines," the university would even aim to become "a world leader in a few selected areas." (p. 1)

Strathclyde's celebration in 1996 of "two hundred years of useful learning" centered on a University Week filled with symbols of what the university had been and had become. The key events were held in a former old church building acquired on the edge of the campus that after much careful and expensive renovation had been transformed into a place for concerts, graduation ceremonies, and universitywide celebrations. A substantial structure, Barony

Hall was refurbished with beautiful stained glass windows that depicted defining features of the university in highly symbolic form. University Week began in Barony with a performance of Haydn's *Creation*. Midweek, on University Day, formal ceremonies in Barony included a visit by Prince Charles to unveil a commemorative plaque and the awarding of five honorary degrees imaginatively distributed among two supporting industrialists, the President of the University of Tokyo, Baroness Tessa Blackstone, Master of Birkbeck College, London, and James MacMillan, a brilliant young Scottish composer of classical music, 36 years old. Then, on the final night of the week, several hundred supporters, administrators, and faculty attended a ball hosted by the Graduates' Association in Barony and danced until midnight in age-old Scottish style. A good time was had by all: emotions flowed in and around a now-beloved institution. The Scottish weather even behaved as expected, drizzling most of the week and raining out entirely an outdoor academic procession.

The celebratory events of that week achieved a rich integrated symbolism of a Scottish place of useful learning that had itself now learned to combine sense and sensibility. Much of the sensibility as well as the sense thus exhibited stemmed from entrepreneurial actions mounted during the previous 15 years. During that period, government support had been reduced to the bare bones of institutional livelihood. The filling out of university character, including cultural symbols and social amenities that had long symbolized British university life, was left to whatever the universities could do for themselves. In developing a much stronger capacity to assert itself, and take care of itself, Strathclyde had shown in more than one way that entrepreneurial behavior was worth the effort.

5

The Chalmers Thrust: Entrepreneurial Autonomy in the Swedish University System

In 1994 the Chalmers University of Technology was reported to have "opted out" of state-controlled higher education in Sweden. In a homogeneous country that for over a half-century had declared higher education a responsibility of central government alone – and in which national goals of "distributive fairness" and "equivalent quality" led toward controlled standardization – the news, as reported internationally, suggested a shocking change. The first reports were an exaggeration: under a 15-year contract with the national Ministry of Education, Chalmers would continue to receive annual state support based on formulas commonly used across all the universities. Other state rules followed. Strong national unions of faculty and support staff did not go away but continued to apply to Chalmers their negotiated definitions of work conditions and employee rights. But the headlines about opting out did contain a large truth: Chalmers had taken up a unique posture. It would now be a separate "foundation," a "foundation university," one-of-a-kind among the universities. It would have a controlling board of its own, to which all income would flow. It would be more autonomous than the other universities, perhaps much like private higher education enterprises elsewhere, freer in how it appointed and rewarded personnel, allocated resources internally, devised programs and courses, and otherwise went about the business of providing research and teaching and opportunities for student learning.

Chalmers became a promising case for this study not for the 1994 decision per se but for my assumption that for one university in Sweden to seek and receive this new deviant status it would have had a particular developmental trajectory, stretching back for a decade or more, which positioned it for this large formal change. The assumption was appropriate: a significant change at Chalmers, as in other universities, required a decade or more, not a year or two, of developmental explanation. The decision had not been a historical accident. So the purpose of my pursuit of this Swedish case was to ascertain what had been done at "CTH" (Chalmers tekniska högskola) since the early 1980s to turn it toward an entrepreneurial posture. That story is a rich one: as at Warwick, Twente, and Strathclyde, we find organizational elements interacting to generate a promising cycle of change. Chalmers also speaks of an existence that began in 1829. How did it start? Was there a genetic imprint ingrained during the following century and a half that also conditioned post-1980 development?

The Old Chalmers

Chalmers is hardly a proper Swedish name, but William Chalmers (1748–1811), of Scottish ancestry, was born in Gothenburg (Göteborg, in Swedish) on the west coast of Sweden and made his fortune late in the eighteenth century as a director of the Swedish East India Company (founded 1731, dissolved 1813). Upon returning home as a wealthy man, after a decade of trading in Calcutta and the Bengal, he resolved to use his resources, talent, and leadership in efforts to bolster the economic development of the Gothenburg region. (Samuelson and Samuelson, 1993) Along with assisting in such direct action as the construction of a useful canal on the west coast, he became intrigued with the idea of developing an educational enterprise that would bring scientific knowledge to bear on economic and social problems of the day. He consulted with well-known scientists and scholars and soon leaned toward the option of establishing a school of useful learning, an "industrial school," that would have a strong scientific base. He specified in his will that half his wealth should go to this purpose; after his death, friends and supporters founded in 1829 the Chalmers Institute (or "school of craft"). This predecessor organization to what later became Chalmers University thus started as a private institution and contained from the beginning a simultaneous orientation to science and industry.

Private and also very small, the institute was not a project to be equated with Sweden's two universities, both ancient – Uppsala (1477) and Lund (1668). Opening with just 29 students, this small private effort to provide technical education for western Sweden grew to a little over 100 in the mid-nineteenth century, to 300 at the beginning of the twentieth century, and to 650 in 1937, an historic date when the institution was officially brought into the Swedish state-owned system of universities and thereby fully transformed from private to public. To become a Swedish "polytechnic" was the original goal: the leading model at the time of this nonuniversity type of advanced education was the École Polytechnique established in the 1790s in Paris. Other similar institutions emerged in the early nineteenth century in such leading cities of Europe as Berlin, Prague, Vienna, Karlsruhe, and Stockholm. At the outset in Gothenburg work was based in the fields of chemical and mechanical engineering. By the end of the century, structural and electrical engineering had been added. (Samuelson and Samuelson, 1993) Its fields fit a local economy in which paper mills, textile plants, and shipbuilding firms loomed large.

With the campus head selected by a controlling board, five successive long-term principals or directors had a strong hand in directing a small staff in what is now defined as "the old Chalmers" (det gamla Chalmers). The fields from which the principals were drawn attest to the commitment to a relatively strong scientific base in what would increasingly be seen as a technical or technological enterprise very different from the comprehensive university model. The first rector (1829–1852), a disciple of Jons Jacob Berzelius, came from chemistry; the second (1852–1881) from physics; the third (1881–1913) from physics and astronomy; the fourth (1913–1933) from mathematics and physics; the fifth (1934–1943), a Chalmers graduate, from civil engineering. (Samuelson and Samuelson, 1993) Chalmers might be a practical place, but it was also steadily incorporating academic values. The march in the early twentieth century to university outlook and performance was slow but steady: in 1900 an institutional commitment to research was written into its statutes; in 1912, the title of professor, to signify one who does research, was used for the first time and given to 13 academics; the right to award the doctoral degree, gained over the opposition of the established universities, was obtained in 1937 at the time of absorption into the state system.

Although formally private, Chalmers received the state's attention almost from the beginning. What was practiced in Stockholm in advanced education, and in the two ancient universities of Uppsala (near Stockholm) and Lund (in southern Sweden), hardly stretched to where Chalmers was plugging away in a small polytechnic framework. Anyone interested in the development of the west coast of Sweden, specifically in the city of Gothenburg and its region, would be interested in more local institutions. The search for regional alternatives led later in Gothenburg to the establishment of a "free academy" that stressed the humanities, languages, and social science, an institution that became first a college and then as it "gradually conformed to the academic patterns and degree requirements of the ancient universities," formally became the comprehensive University of Gothenburg in 1954. (Geiger, 1986, p. 135) To help Chalmers, the governor of the local region regularly served as chairman of the controlling board. As early as 1836, just a few years after the institution opened its doors, the King of Sweden, a representative of Napoleon, helped out with a state subsidy that set a pattern of regular state contributions. Thus, Chalmers developed over a long period of time as a private-public mixture, a blend that undoubtedly eased the transition in the 1930s into full state-supported status. Perhaps "almost everything started private" in the city and region of Gothenburg, as various Chalmers administrators and faculty remarked in interviews, but little in education would escape the eye of an aggressive state, especially when expanding schools and universities outran the resources available through private donation.

Sweden became rich after World War II. One scholar remarked that "our industry was intact and everyone wanted to buy from us." With state ministries harnessed to expanding national ambitions, Sweden was an early forerunner among European countries in the transition from elite to mass higher education. The late 1950s and the 1960s were a golden age for founding new institutions and greatly expanding old ones. The University of Gothenburg, for example, formed in the early 1950s largely by the merger of a university college and a school of medicine, increased from about 500 students at the end of the 1940s to over 20,000 at the end of the 1960s. (University of Gothenburg, 1996, p. 4) The demand was there and the state was happy to provide a modernized educational structure that would provide the human capital for a Swedish "middle way" between the West and the East. Compared to counterparts in France and Germany, Swedish universities could somewhat control their individual size: most simply flowed with the demand. But in specialized universities focused on engineering and applied science, the high cost of buildings, equipment, and laboratories operates as a brake on unceasing expansion. While the University of Gothenburg continued to grow in a major way to a size in the 1990s of over 30,000 full- and part-time students, nearby Chalmers increased to only about 5,000 to 6,000 students. In typical European style the local comprehensive university spread out geographically over the city. Chalmers remained a unified campus and added a small number of adjacent buildings as the expansion of fields and faculty and student numbers crowded the old facilities.

At the end of the 1970s, Chalmers could be characterized as a small, relatively focused institution of higher education that could claim a certain instinct for a "private" sense of autonomy. After the 1994 transition to a foundation status, those knowledgeable about the institutional history could speak of long-term swings in control from private to state and back toward private. The concentration on engineering and applied science had also been congenial for both rectorial leadership and industrial contact. But still, in 1980, Chalmers was not autonomous in any internationally meaningful sense of the term. The state provided its funds: a national rule book governed its operations. What did happen in this corner of Gothenburg was that small experiments in organizational development got underway that were to help pave the way toward the large one-of-a-kind "breakaway" of 1994.

The 1980–1995 Transformation

The linkage among the five transforming elements identified in this study is so close at Chalmers that a circle of interaction can be analytically entered from any one of them. Beginning in the late 1970s, *the academic heartland* played a leading role when the leading campus academic announced his commitment to innovation and began a line of activity that in time most fully embodied and expressed entrepreneurship at Chalmers and, arguably, in the entire Swedish university system. This up-from-the-bottom initiative was avidly backed by an *administrative core* that was then being strengthened and would persist throughout the 1980s with a strong two-person cadre of rector and administrator director. The bottom-up and top-down forms of steering initiative shared a commitment to *an institutional idea* that Chalmers would become a more entrepreneurial institution, one that, as later put, would have "a plurality of special places for innovative behavior." Those places soon composed a complex *developmental periphery* in which new units would be largely project oriented and interdisciplinary. Bridging to industrial firms and other outside groups, they brought outside definitions of problems into the university and threw such formal lines of outreach as spin-off firms and science-park affiliations across traditional university boundaries. Along the way, changes in *income streams* followed and played their own stimulating role.

I begin with matters of the *academic heartland*. Professor J.T. Wallmark was an internationally renowned scientist and inventor in electronics who, after spending productive years in the United States working for RCA (Radio Corporation of America), returned to his homeland in the mid-1960s. He again spent some time in the U.S., then came back permanently to Sweden as chair and head of department in solid-state physics within Chalmers School of Electrical Engineering. His American experience had instilled in him much admiration for a spirit of industrial inventiveness, which seemed to be lacking in Sweden. He attempted at Chalmers to develop a commitment to innovative behavior, even provide inspirational leadership for it. To explore the possibilities for students and young faculty to create their own companies, he began to experiment with the generation of spin-off companies, particularly as organized by his own students. The university arranged a "new personal chair" for him, designated for "Innovation Engineering," that made a strong symbolic statement. As stressed later in interviews with leaders of that period: "he had an impact on everybody at the university. Here was a respected professor changing his field to highlight 'innovation'." In 1979, he started up the Chalmers Innovation Center (CIC) – a critical step in building a *developmental periphery* – as a bit of infrastructure that would systemically advance "the transfer of new product ideas and new technology from university to industry." (Chalmers University of Technology, 1994, 1995) A university incubator building on campus was opened in 1983 to house the growing number of spin-off firms. Two additional buildings later had to be utilized, as the development of spin-offs continued and fed off itself, under Wallmark and then under his successor, Sören Sjölander (1991- –), who was also very entrepreneurial and was respected in industry. In 1995, a greatly enlarged building was being planned that would house both the CIC and a larger number of new offshoot companies. By this time CIC could boast of having assisted at the birth of over 200 such companies. As early as 1986, CIC also had underway a "seed capital" (venture capital) firm that could provide risk capital and managerial advice for the new companies. A CIC Business Advisory Board was formalized in the early 1990s; a business development program for the spin-offs was launched in 1994. One step led to another in a highly entrepreneurial fashion.

CIC also established an Industrial Contact Group as early as 1983 to draw in companies that might be interested in learning about research activities and consulting services at Chalmers as well as about the progress of spin-offs. Membership in the mid-1990s included many large firms that have dominated the Sweden economy, from Astra Hässle in pharmaceuticals, to Ericsson in electronics, to SAAB in transportation, to SKF, the bearer of ball-bearings to the world. The CIC developed an academic base in the Department of Innovation Engineering and Management, from which it drew its personnel (only departments had the power of appointment).

Further, special undergraduate courses have been developed around the theme of "Innovation in Practice," and a brief graduate course has been offered to the public and to undergraduates in patenting. Business attorneys have been lined up to give legal advice to inventors and spin-offs free of charge. And only slightly to one side, with much the same leadership, Chalmers has built a set of high level management training programs (CHAMPS) that take top Swedish executives off to meet leading experts in other countries as well as bring an international faculty to local sessions. The executive leadership effort includes "company-specific programs." (Chalmers University of Technology, 1995–96) CHAMPS is a notable tub-on-its-own-bottom, able to charge high fees for its high-flying courses, first class all the way, that large firms willingly afford for their senior or would-be senior managers.

A *strengthened steering core* also played an important part in backing such efforts. Top-down initiative to move Chalmers toward a dynamic entrepreneurial posture followed from the central leadership of a rector and administrative director. Sven Olving, an electronics expert with some industrial background and experience in American universities, who had been an active vice-rector for seven years (1966–1973), took over as rector in 1974 and continued until 1989 – 23 years in top administration. Familiar with the style of command common in industrial firms, Olving was willing to be a "CEO" (chief executive officer), even a "boss." In 1980 he brought in Folke Hjalmers to serve with him as a similarly spirited administrative director, a position often filled in Sweden and in Europe by legally trained administrators who normally closely follow national rulebooks and conservatively guard public monies. Olving and Hjalmers pushed hard at the traditional academic divisions and departments to be more self-assertive. They used, in an early stage, "program budgeting" to force greater responsibility and accountability at the lower levels. As a specialized institution centered on engineering, Chalmers was seen nationally as a "single faculty" university. Swedish statistics, for example, show eight faculties at Uppsala, six at Gothenburg, and one at Chalmers. (Lane, 1992, p. 690) Major subunits at Chalmers were then designated as schools, instead of the more common faculties. In the early 1980s just six of these major units existed: (chemical, civil, electrical, and mechanical engineering, engineering physics, and architecture). A Department of Mathematics grew into a School of Mathematics and Computing Sciences by the end of the decade. The schools were chaired by deans. The move to decentralized budgeting greatly strengthened their positions and turned them into major players, a point to which we will return. The vigorous Olving administration also played a key role in the early development of a science park at Chalmers and especially in supporting the Wallmark-led CIC. The rector worked assiduously to retain Wallmark at Chalmers; he appointed him to the special chair and backed his innovation moves to the hilt. The 1980s central administration was also deeply involved in additional components of the developmental periphery discussed below; for example, the university's early move toward European Community projects.

But as we have seen at Warwick, Twente, and Strathclyde – and will soon observe in Joensuu – a highly personal form of rectorial leadership can generally serve only for a time as an agency of change in a European university. Chair-based professors expect to exercise strong authority: their historic senate remains in the picture. As academics uncomfortable with dictates from above push back, more collegial forms of leadership reassert themselves. In 1991, with the ascendance of Anders Sjöberg to the rectorship/presidency, a more collegial group formed up at the center to represent the overall institutional interest. Evolving during the first half of the 1990s, this more collegial center became an inner ring of seven to eight, consisting of the rector, three-to-four selected (not elected) vice-rectors, and three senior administrative officers. An enlarged ring brought in the nine deans of the schools: a School of Environmental Sciences and a School of Industrial Production and Economics (later to be a School of Technology Management and Economics) had been added to the seven identified above. As the deans were increasingly incorporated into overall university steering, the group thus formed is reminiscent of the University Management Group at Strathclyde. With this greater circle involving 16 or more key players, the strengthened administrative core had become much more a matter of collective leadership.

But at the same time, in contrast to traditional academic style, the newly evolved central group was and is relatively managerial. The rector-president is clearly number one; he selects the vice-rectors, rather than having to accept elected representatives; the three administrative officers clearly fall under his office; and, most important, the deans have become managers of the basic academic components, responsible for budget and initiatives in their particular realms. They become key people as they take on the role of classic middle managers in business firms. A clear arm of overall management in a chain of command, they are also close to the working staff and act to represent them up the line. And, as in the evolving Strathclyde structure, the deans at Chalmers have become central in the reconciliation of new managerial values with traditional academic ones, *and* in the linkage between overall institutional interests and the separate interests of major internal segments. Their involvement at the center helps to turn them into representatives of the entire institution.

Picking up again with the *developmental periphery*: Chalmers has developed a major science park adjacent to its campus. Initiated in 1984 under the triple sponsorship of the university, local city government, and a regional chamber of commerce, and opened for business in a new large building in 1987, the park has been primarily a place in which business firms can locate research activities that can possibly benefit from the university environment. It is self-defined as "a true science park in that it is populated by research units from private companies. Activities focus on applied research and not on development. . . The current tenants are mainly research departments and specialized companies from groups including Volvo, SKF, SCA and Celsius and also high-tech spin-off companies from Chalmers." (Chalmers Institute of Technology, 1994) The university sees the park as a key component in an emerging "Göteborg Technopole," with the Faculty of Natural Sciences at the University of Gothenburg joining Chalmers and the park to constitute the second largest "university town in Sweden for natural sciences and technology research." By 1995 plans to double the park's size were well underway: late afternoon observation of rock blasting to clear an adjacent site was an unscheduled treat during my second visit in September-October 1996.

"The plurality of places" for new outward-oriented activities at Chalmers, beyond the innovation center and the science park, each with manifold arms, received another major boost in the mid-1990s with the initiation of a half-dozen "Competence Centers." The new centers are part of a national effort of the Swedish National Board for Industrial and Technical Development (NUTEK) to stimulate strategic research in conjunction with industry and the universities. Undertaken as a ten-year venture, the organizing agreement for each center specifies three way funding in which the university chiefly provides space and personnel while NUTEK and industry put up the cash. This type of university unit, firmly based on industry involvement, is heavily project oriented, hence generally interdisciplinary, and incorporates industrial definitions of problems. In a competition that started out with over 300 applications in 1992–1993, six centers out of an emerging national total of 28 to 30 were awarded to Chalmers, in such specialties as higher velocity technology (an area within telecommunications) and catalysis, centered on catalytic combustion and emission filtration. (Chalmers University of Technology, 1994–95, pp. 19–20)

Experts at the university see this new organizational form as possibly "unique to Sweden" in Europe, and that working "this close to industry" really amounted to "a new type of research." Each center has its own board of directors, with joint participation and responsibility all the way: "What is most promising with this new approach is that researchers from the university as well as representatives from business and industry together formulate the strategically important research programmes, assuming collective responsibility for financing and execution. Further, this organisational form allows straightforward interaction between business and industry representatives in that they can take part in joint projects run by the competence centres." (p. 20) The director of each center at Chalmers is free to explore within the university, without asking the permission of deans and department heads, for relevant personnel who might be willing to commit to an industrially defined project and work with researchers from industry. The new Competence Center for Catalysis, for example, soon involved professors from three university departments and researchers from six firms working on each of two major projects. The young, research-capable director was able immediately to bring in a half-dozen Ph.D. students – NUTEK money was important in their support – and was planning to increase their ranks to 15 in two years. More permanent researchers were also expected to become core staff. Applications from students were already seen as excellent, since they could sense "a good road to industry." The center could help pave a new career path: its doctoral students, while cheek-to-jowl with researchers from industry, would not work at the firm-specific level. They would position themselves "back a step from marketable products," on broader problems common to an industry sector. The problems of cleaning up exhaust emission, for example, were obviously important – and virtually inexhaustible!

An early finding from the new competence centers was that knowledge transfer could flow from industry to the university as much as the other way around. The specific problem-solving technical knowledge of researchers in firms frequently exceeds that of related university researchers. Such input to university know-how will undoubtedly grow within university-industry relations as more industrial firms build research staffs highly competent in sector-specific as well as firm-specific knowledge and technique.

The developmental periphery at Chalmers also came to include two other major components that were decidedly uncommon among Swedish universities; alumni relations and fundraising. European universities have generally not defined their graduates as "alumni." Graduates owed no particular loyalty to the university that trained them; the university, in turn, did not formally organize the graduates as a support group. But stemming from its initial privateness, as early as the mid-1800s alumni-type groups formed up at Chalmers as amateur-run voluntary associations. In recent decades, certain features of student life, discussed below, caused student leaders to be closely attached to the university while on campus and strongly disposed them to identify with one another and Chalmers in general after graduation. They became an important "club," with close interpersonal ties, especially in the Gothenburg area but also throughout Sweden. Particularly in light of the more independent status of "foundation university," the university in the 1990s has sought to contact graduates and organize them as an alumni group, building upon the voluntary associations already in place. Their moral support, and beyond that their financial support for an independent Chalmers, was needed. In whatever form, alumni-type identification among graduates is a valuable resource at Chalmers, apparently at a level unique among Swedish universities.

Chalmers has also started down the path of formal fundraising, with a campaign that started up in the mid-1990s and was spearheaded by a new Office for Fundraising and Alumni Affairs, located in the science park and headed by an American of proven ability in such activity. Chalmers has long received individual donations from private benefactors and industrial firms anxious to support the development of particular fields of expertise. Other Swedish universities have also increasingly done so: the University of Gothenburg was able to develop a major business school after receiving a large donation from a private benefactor for a new, architecturally eye-catching complex of buildings. But Chalmers overall stands out in commitment to develop this particular type of outreach. Its ties to industry and to alumni provide a base for doing so. As seen by its staff, Stockholm has government but Gothenburg – "the second city" – has industry, whose leaders smile kindly upon a local enterprise focused almost single-mindedly on the training of engineers and other applied scientists, particularly one now so mindful of innovation and industrial competence. The university has also worked hard to develop a sturdy relationship with the development-minded European Union (EU). An office of Brussels-contact experts operates under a vice-president for development. In the mid-1990s Chalmers could point to an annual total of 100 EU contracts. Its habit of looking outward in Sweden has readily moved to the all-Europe level.

Through its EU contacts, and going beyond, Chalmers has strongly operationalized its "internationalization" through cooperative agreements in research. The EU provides a base: "A typical EU research project includes 5–7 partners from 4–5 countries. These partners can be small or large industries, universities or research institutes who wish, through concerted action, to tackle a problem relevant to business and industry or to society." Further: "during the past five years, international collaboration has changed character from regular, unregulated cooperation to cooperation regulated by different forms of agreements, the latter totaling 450." The regulated agreements had increased by more than 100 percent in a five-year period. All schools were involved, and the formal agreements stretched beyond western and eastern Europe to the United States, Asia, Australia, Africa, and South America. To promote "contacts with foreign centers of excellence," signed agreements of coopera- tion were worked out during 1994–1995 with the California Institute of Technology ("Cal Tech"), the famous ETH in Zurich, and France's legendary École Polytechnique. (Chalmers University of Technology, 1994–95, pp. 20–21) The "regulated" research agreement had become a powerful tool for firmly establishing international collaboration "as an integral part of the research activities." It also helps to thoroughly fuse the developmental periphery of the university with virtually all of its academic heartland.

To return once more to the *academic heartland*: students are integrated with the campus administration at Chalmers and brought squarely into the entrepreneurial ethos by certain regularized practices of student leadership. The student union has a parliament that chooses its own officers for the following year (a common feature in Swedish universities). Then Chalmers has arranged for four to five or more of the officers each year to be on full-time status; they are given a salary and freed from studies for one year. They are expected to take a year longer to complete their work for the first degree, normally four and one-half to five years. Such officers are closely linked to the campus administration as they in effect become junior administrators; they are allowed to participate in many administration-faculty committees. Good students have been attracted to these leadership posts, and their intensive, paid involvement leads them toward close identification with the character of the institution.

Several faculty and administrators who had served in these posts when they were students spoke, in interviews, of a stronger corporate identity at Chalmers than at other Swedish universities: a "spirit of Chalmers" based on close cooperation among student leaders, faculty, and administration. Those who had served as student union officers remembered with pride that they fought for the status and autonomy of the university. They recalled, for example, twice joining the effort to avoid merging Chalmers with the much larger, comprehensive University of Gothenburg. Full-time student leaders have also typically been central players in a small, self-selecting student campus group – a "Skull-and-Bones" type – that by "tapping" about a hundred students each year had led to a distinctive and highly focused alumni grouping of some three to four thousand graduates that "has its arms out all over Sweden" and has generated other alumni-type associations. Graduates who were leaders in the student union in their undergraduate days get together periodically to celebrate their common identity.

University staff most familiar with the student leadership-to-alumni linkage portray it as "a middle point of the Chalmers spirit." Part of this connection has been the large Chalmers Engineers Association, with about 11,000 paying members out of 24,000 graduates. For those thereby linked in a plurality of small and large associations, you "keep this relationship [to other Chalmerites] all your life." It all starts back in student life, in campus student groups and similar ones, cut on a smaller scale, in the separate schools. Faculty and administrators knowledgeable about American practices likened the spirit thus generated to that often noted among students and graduates in small private colleges and universities in the United States. Here the student culture even includes a "special relationship to Gothenburg": an annual parade each May by the students through the central streets of the city gives the entire city a chance to see "the spirit" in action.

At Chalmers, then, the academic heartland and developmental periphery are considerably fused around the institutional idea of an entrepreneurial university. The idea is strongly embodied in a host of campus structures and tangible practices; a "can-do spirit" extends well into student life. The idea has broadened into an ethos, a culture reaching across disparate administrative offices, outreach units, academic departments, and research centers. Evident in ordinary operations, the sense of entrepreneurship is widespread.

Our fifth element, *a discretionary funding base*, has played a less determining role than at Warwick, Twente, and Strathclyde. But it is not unimportant historically, and since 1994 it has become a central item. Like other Swedish universities, Chalmers has been heavily dependent on government financing from a mainline ministry. Alert to the need for human capital, the national government has been relatively generous to the higher education system, both in supporting first-degree work, largely free of student fees, and especially in supporting academic research. The government openly specifies that about one-third of university assistance is for undergraduate education and two-thirds is for research and advanced training. Numerous research councils offer a second line of income, and other governmental departments enter the picture – significantly for a science and engineering university – especially national bodies that support development of trade, industry, and technology. In contrast to Germany and France, where substantial research monies are allocated to research institutes outside universities, Sweden has put such funds inside them.

Using the previously described three-stream breakdown of university income, "core support" at Chalmers dropped from about 67 percent in 1980 to 55 percent in 1995. The picture after 1990 is muddled by some major changes in allocations after 1994, for example, an allotment for the costs of premises was included for the first time. Income from research councils, already a substantial item at about one-fifth of total resources in 1980, rose to about 25 percent. Monies from the third stream, "all other sources," rose from about 14 to 20 percent. The second and third streams together, representing nonguaranteed funds raised largely by competitive effort, approximated 45 percent. Income diversification has been underway, even in a national setting where core support for universities has been relatively generous.

Income figures for 1994–1995 showed undergraduate programs to be fully supported by state subsidy. For "Ph.D. programmes and research" such support amounted to only about one-third of the total, with "external means" becoming the main support. (Chalmers University of Technology, 1994–95, p. 61) The "external" included both our second and third streams: research councils and noneducation government departments, where fundraising is competitive; and two other sources, "commissioned research" and "contributions, funds, gifts," the latter coming from Swedish private foundations and industrial firms willing to contribute both earmarked and unearmarked funds for the long-term welfare of Chalmers. The Wallenberg Foundation is an

TABLE 5–1

Sources of Financial Support, Chalmers University of Technology, 1980–1995

(millions of Swedish kroner)

Year	Core Support		Research Councils		All Other Sources		Total	
	Amount	Percent	Amount	Percent	Amount	Percent	Amount	Percent
1980	222	67	62	19	47	14	331	100
1985	315	59	104	20	113	21	532	100
1990	618	58	258	24	193	18	1069	100
1995	794*	55	353	25	290	20	1437	100

*Under the new 1994 "Foundation" arrangement, a governmental allotment for costs of premises was included for the first time.
Source: Trend data compiled by Helen Strömberg, Chalmers Planning Office

important contributor to Swedish universities generally. Their major gifts tend to be for buildings and equipment; industrial firms also contributed in this fashion at Chalmers, particularly for expensive equipment needed by departments and faculties.

Thus, much institutional development took place at Chalmers that we can see as a run-up to 1994, the year of the widely noted "opt-out" from the general university system. The five pathways of transformation captured in this study converged to become a predisposition (not evident at Swedish comprehensive universities) to take the bold but risky step of seeking and obtaining a more independent status. The institution had an historical sense, a cultural component, that it had once been private and could again take up a somewhat private status: it could survive and even prosper without being a "state university." Its administrative core, long disposed to rectorial leadership, had been measurably strengthened in the 1980s and early 1990s by the location of authority in certain positions – rector, dean, department head – and by a pro-active form of collegial managerialism in a central steering group. The idea of entrepreneurial behavior was increasingly in favor, promulgated both from the academic heartland and the central administration: Professor Wallmark was the flesh-and-blood defining figure, the Chalmers Innovation Center a defining unit. A developmental periphery blossomed into a virtually self-propelling array of initiatives in the CIC, the science park, EC-project arrangements, competence centers, alumni linkages, and fundraising. The periphery and the heartland became indistinguishable from one another in the whole-hearted acceptance of the social and academic legitimacy of entrepreneurship. What better way to serve the nation when Swedish industry needed all the help it could get?

The idea of one or more universities taking up a "foundation" status was a product of a conservative-party government (1991–1994) that was considerably more interested in the promotion of free enterprise and exposure of public enterprises to competitive forces than had been true of the social democratic party long in power. Separately incorporated foundations funded or assisted by state money were pushed along two lines. First, new national research foundations for the support of strategic research were created out of "wage earners funds," a hotly debated move and one later vigorously contested when the social democratic party returned to power in 1995. The second was broached formally by the government in late 1991. Universities were asked – as part of a broader effort to decentralize control and stimulate their realm – whether they were interested in turning themselves into foundations, to be run essentially like private institutions in the same legal form as "limited companies." State universities would become foundation universities that would receive a large lump-sum allocation at the outset to constitute an endowment, enter into a 15-year contract with the government that stipulated general targets of performance and guaranteed annual support from the state, and then proceed to operate under their own boards of control and management to more freely allocate resources internally.

The proffered status was difficult for most Swedish universities to accept: all the comprehensive ones soon backed away, preferring to remain in the traditional legal and cultural framework. If the current system was not broken, and it clearly was not, why take such a drastic step? The diffuse comprehensive places readily saw the move as difficult to implement. Just the effort to convince the semi-independent faculties that stretched from medicine to the humanities would seemingly take an endless amount of time and promote too much discord. When the plan became narrowed to the notion of one such experimental enterprise at the university level, the contest to obtain this status narrowed to the country's two technological universities, Chalmers and the Royal Institute of Technology in Stockholm. Chalmers was chosen as the institution best oriented and administered to make the change. (A university college in Jönköping also received the new status.) Two years of anticipatory discussion within the university had led to the conclusion that it could prosper under the new arrangement.

Why did Chalmers wish to make "a transition to a foundation?" In a brief submitted to the government in 1993, three reasons were given: it wanted to gain "simultaneous right of disposition over all resources," from funds for physical plant construction to weekly wages for part-time staff; it wanted "a more flexible organisation" and "less restrictive handling of finances," to have "greater opportunity for our own organisational and financial initiatives"; and it wanted to have "greater flexibility when it comes to recruiting and employing staff ": (Chalmers University of Technology, 1993, p. 1) The university declared its ambition to be an international leader "in the field of technical education and research," and specifically "to become one of the ten best universities of technology in Europe." (p. 2) The Chalmers brief argued that here was a Swedish university exceptionally prepared for what would be an exciting opportunity but also a possibly wrenching change.

Highlighting "the Chalmers spirit" as a "feeling of fellowship with the university which is shared by students and staff alike," the university stressed its developmental background:

> For many years now, CTH has been working in this spirit with a view to obtaining more flexible organizational and financial solutions and also has long traditions when it comes to developing new organizational forms and financial systems. . . . CTH has focused special attention on the question of developing management functions and leadership. CTH has also worked to obtain a more flexible appointments systems. CTH is therefore very well equipped for the transition to a foundation and this offers excellent potential for a rapid effect on the development of CTH after a transition. (p. 3)

Or, as the president put it, after the deed was done:

> The idea of the foundation conforms unusually well with the very long tradition at Chalmers of working towards increased independence and searching for independent solutions. We want to do things 'ourselves.' We want to 'assert ourselves.' (Chalmers University of Technology, 1995)

The president went on to point out that the independence of foundation status would give Chalmers the opportunity to (a) create a recruitment system and career structure that would give it a better chance of recruiting top researchers from abroad, (b) develop different admission procedures for students, and (c) achieve greater staff movement between the university and industry. The "new conditions for revitalization," if "correctly managed," would give Chalmers "unique potential." It will probably take five to ten years to see how well these "opportunities" fare. After twelve to eighteen months under the new status, central administrators were optimistic. To begin with: "we do not have to ask Stockholm before we do something"; "we do not have to read paragraphs in a rulebook" that pertain to conditions holding "in Uppsala and Lund but not in Gothenburg." Chalmers would now have "its own book of rules" unique to its own character and context. The greater leeway in faculty recruitment and faculty career structure inside the university seemed highly promising: Chalmers could here make its own rules, and its choices among candidates for faculty positions could not be challenged, as they could be and were in the state universities, by those not selected; appointments could be sped along; criteria for faculty promotion could give more weight, if desired, to strong undergraduate teaching.

Most of all, the steering capacity of the university at the all-campus level in particular, but also at the individual-school level, promised from the outset of the new status to be leaner, more sophisticated, and more adaptive. A new top board of directors of fewer than ten people – the Foundation Board – was seen as replacing the state as owner. Major industrial executives became members and one took on the key post of chairman. The university president sits on this board, but not as chair – an important matter. All income legally flows to this top board. Under it at a second major level, a new entity, the

Chalmers University of Technology Limited, has its own larger (about 15) board of directors, also chaired by a leading industrialist, with representatives from among the ranks of faculty, students, employee organizations, municipal commissioners, and chairmen/presidents of such leading Swedish firms as Saab, Astra Hassle, and ABB, the European electrical giant. Again, the university president is a member but does not chair. Instead, "on the authority of the board" the president "is responsible for the executive management." Grouped under the president are the vice-presidents and central administrators, described earlier as the inner ring of a strengthened administrative core, now defined as "the University's Central Management Group." (Chalmers University of Technology, 1994–95, p. 60) Faculty are represented among the vice-presidents.

At the internal-school level, steering boards are chaired by an outsider who then takes up a position of influence alongside the dean. A "window" was thereby opened, in the early opinion of some central administrators: "before, the Dean was alone: now he has someone beside him"; we get "two people from different backgrounds and experience going into matters."

Top administrators at Chalmers saw the new chair of the board at both university and school levels as key in making an evermore dynamic university more open to environmental influences. Top industrialists not willing to waste time could now be persuaded to take up these active posts. With their considerable personal influence they would be able to convince other top people to serve and take turns in active assignments. The introduction of sharp eyes and active approaches to management was soon evident.

The foundation device so much favored by the conservative government of the early 1990s fell into disfavor under a social democratic government that returned to power in 1995. What the previous minister of education and science had seen as compelling decentralization and stimulating competition the new minister saw as the introduction of "chaos": the once well-integrated university system had become a "mess" (*Times Higher Education Supplement,* 1996, p. 11) The major research foundations were portrayed as receiving an inappropriate redistribution of funds. *And* there should be no more Chalmers-type breakouts: one was enough, and its governance should tilt back toward the state orbit. The minister chipped away at its new independence: Chalmers could not buy its property from the state, as originally negotiated, but could only rent it; some state representatives might be added to the university board of directors. For all the universities, the minister voiced the threat of a major reduction in funding for *basic* research equal to the *strategic* research monies they were now obtaining from the new research foundations. The rectors' association expressed profound dissatisfaction with the minister's "recentralizing moves": "It seems that Mr. Tham [the education minister] is overly fond of regulations." (p. 11) The whole issue of state regulation and university autonomy was again up for reconsideration, with Chalmers seen by social democratic government officials as the extreme case of what had gone wrong. A Swedish-style consultative "dialogue" took on a sharp tone: the social democratic minister was publicly branded a "fool" by his predecessor for targeting the government's basic research investment for cuts of up to 50 percent: "Small countries with high ambitions can't afford to make these kinds of cuts." (*Science*, 1995, p. 1901)

The conservative government worked hard while in power to lock in the new foundation structures against any later social democratic efforts to wipe them out and restore the status quo ante. In 1996 Chalmers felt its foundation status would remain basically intact, even if successive ministers and parliaments were to nibble here and there. The legal status seemed basically firm; friends in Sweden's large firms were strong allies; the university had deep roots in its west coast area; and even the Gothenburg "second-city" sentiment helped as a basis for local support. Foundation status seemed promising and worth fighting for. It clearly meant enhanced autonomy. It extended funding possibilities. It promoted stronger self-steering. An already enterprising university had positioned itself to be even more entrepreneurial.

Conclusion

The old Chalmers that developed during the many decades between the 1830s and the 1970s manifested certain features that aided a later transformation. A slowly developing institution acquired a memory of private origin and leadership. Concentrated on technology, it became more inclined than Sweden's comprehensive universities to link up with industry and to incorporate some business-like habits. Yet, after its absorption into the state system of higher education in the 1930s, it had undergone much state-led standardization. In what became the Swedish top-down model of planning and developing public activities, state authorities played a central role in composing an integrated and planned university system. Throughout "the accent was on uniformity as the guarantee for maintaining equal standards." (Organisation for Economic Co-operation and Development (OECD), 1995, p. 185) Regularized, Chalmers behaved as a national public university shaped by the high value placed on equity and homogeneity in Swedish government and society. Business firms might innovate and compete, but universities in a growing welfare state cooperated with ministers and their staffs in the furthering of a public service.

Some breathing space to move in the opposite direction – toward "competition and choice" – developed slowly throughout the Swedish public sector beginning in the late 1970s. (pp. 185–188) By the end of the 1980s decentralization of control in the university sector, from state to university, was heralded as a basic trend. (Lane, 1992; Elzinga, 1993) Decentralization per se, however, was no guarantee of local institutional initiative. Longstanding internal divisions of resources among faculties and departments, faculty and support staff, had become inflexible sunk costs. Authority was diffused among autonomous parts. An active posture would need new mechanisms of steerage and stimulation. Organizations not long accustomed to self-steering faced many internal roadblocks in developing new capacities for institution building.

Steps taken at Chalmers during the 1980s and early 1990s were at the cutting edge of such institutional change in Swedish universities. Innovative behavior became prized in the institution's academic heartland as much as in its central administration. Contacts with large industrial firms were worked out in a multiplicity of new university units. At the same time the university systematically pursued the generation and growth of small and medium-size firms in high technology. Strong rectorial leadership arose in a highly personal form and then settled down in a more collegial central management group. Students as well as young faculty were encouraged to become entrepreneurs. "Can do" became a byword. As industrial leaders were increasingly drawn into the governance structure of the university, it was encouraged to be more businesslike. A universitywide predisposition to be an enterprising place, gradually created over a 15-year period, then led to a growing willingness in the early 1990s to take up the highly unusual status of a foundation university and thereby become one-of-a-kind. This major step made the institution significantly a private enterprise even as it maintained membership in the overall system of public universities. Chalmers became in this hybrid sense somewhat similar to the Stockholm School of Economics and the Karolinska Institute (in medicine), prized units of Swedish higher education which receive government monies but at the same time exist in a more independent status than the mainline comprehensive universities. In this new status, Chalmers became in effect a Swedish experiment – a pilot institution given the opportunity to see what could be done anew when a university ventured further down the road of independence.

At the heart of the derived Chalmers posture is a determination to break down old walls erected around traditional departments and schools. New primary structures have been introduced that cut across traditional lines and bring in external definitions of problems and subjects. Chalmers has become a significant experiment in university matrix organization in which new nondepartmental points of view are given organizational footing. Outward-looking interdisciplinary research centers, project-centered, are given space at the table. Most clearly in the new competence centers, such units can even have their own directors who have considerable authority to choose priorities, establish projects, obtain financing, and assemble personnel. The leaders of these centers even report directly to the rector rather than to faculty and department heads. Such units reach to industry as much as to traditional segments of the university, and virtually constitute a mediating third party. They bring outside points of view squarely into the operational structure. Taken together as a new infrastructure, they constitute a systematic way to form new competencies. Other institutions have become increasingly aware of their advantages: in 1996 they were becoming a major segment of internal organization in at least four other Swedish universities.

The status of foundation university, now undergoing testing at Chalmers after its introduction in 1994, is worthy of international attention. As a hybrid institutional form that leaves a university broadly influenced by state authority, and partially supported by state money under long-term contracts, it takes up a quasi-private status that guarantees more fiscal and managerial autonomy. The foundation mechanism offers public universities the possibility of recovering much of the autonomy they had when higher education had an elite status and a small university system was a low-cost item in governmental budgets; then officials could, with some trust and not too much concern, "leave the money on the stump." Under latter-day conditions of a greatly expanded and much more costly system, long-term contracts between state and university can again offer significant operational autonomy. The greater freedom can then become the ground for active university self-development. The means for doing so developed at Chalmers by the interacting elements highlighted in this study.

The hard work of moving universities into enterprising postures is not for everyone. But for those who make the effort, and at least partially succeed, the struggle offers large payoffs. As in all four universities we have thus far reviewed, new sources of revenue can be found and made a regular part of income. A portfolio of extra sources can turn "soft money" into dependable financing, even as the former "hard money" of state allocations becomes soggy. The university on its own can experiment with new infrastructures that may be highly valuable if not essential for future sustainability. On its own it can actively cross-subsidize across old and new lines of activity, from fields that readily bring in revenue to ones that do not. It can shut down departments that are terminally ill rather than let them linger on to undergo death "by a thousand cuts." It can introduce more flexibility in career lines and work-load assignments.

Most important, an enterprising outlook can measurably strengthen a university's overall identity. The "idea of the university" on which academics in many countries lovingly dwell, with memories of the days of old, becomes a specified developing idea of a particular university. As the idea becomes operationally defined and elaborated in an institutional culture, integrative identity emerges. The assertion of distinctiveness at Chalmers offers a valuable sense of place. Its belief system adds intrinsic rewards to those found in teaching and research; shared rewards add meaning to the academic life. From a distance observers might assume that this technological university is a coldly rational place and that alone. But up close it emerges as a university that goes beyond its valuable engineering-type rationality. Deepened by a will to be assertedly and even aggressively distinctive, its sense of an institutional self offers much more to faculty, administrators, students, and others drawn into its daily activities. We find entrepreneurship recreating community.

6

The Joensuu Reform: Piloting Decentralized Control in Finnish Universities

Located in the northern periphery of European higher education, the modest University of Joensuu in rural Finland has come a long way in a short time. A new university of the 1960s, it took up a special role in the late 1980s that led to a strong assertion of distinctiveness. Its progress on a new pathway of development has made it an appropriate case for this study. Notably, to steer that effort, central figures at the university scoured the international literature for ideas that would allow them to link "theory" to "practice." They conceptualized their framework and their findings in a series of papers presented at conferences in Western and Eastern Europe and as far away as Africa. They highlighted from experience a Finnish conception of what "an entrepreneurial university," a "self-regulative" institution, could be. (Hölttä and Pulliainen, 1993; Hölttä, 1995)

The Joensuu case also brought the study back to the world of comprehensive universities. University entrepreneurship ought not be seen as a phenomenon limited to technological universities or to large comprehensive ones that have built major ties to industry. National and local conditions variously constrain what I call later "the entrepreneurial response." Always relative to context, the response is fashioned from possibilities arising from the interaction of organizational capabilities with environmental limitations and openings. Capability includes the will, the mounted determination, to fashion a major remodeling. Let us examine how this particular small place found the will to change and how it then worked out ways to strengthen its character to face an uncertain future.

A Regional University in Karelia

To become a somewhat comprehensive university, especially an innovative one, the University of Joensuu did not have much going for it at the outset. Officially born in 1969, it represented in the beginning the "upgrading" of teacher education from a predecessor teachers college, a move taken by the national government throughout the Finnish higher education system at the time to put the education of all public school teachers into a more academic mold. The new university also started out quite small, with just four professors/associate professors and 145 students in the first year, and was planned to remain a small outpost, much in the form of a "university college," with a target size of 2,000 students a decade down the road. No multiversity was projected, no serious rival to the old Finnish universities in Helsinki and Turku in magnitude of subjects, faculty, and students was envisioned. As part of a countrywide regionalization of higher education, the university was also clearly earmarked to be a "regional university," with the education of teachers for local schools and other regional services to be undertaken in the province of Karelia, a particularly poor region of Finland, bordered on the east by the USSR and surrounded by huge areas of forests and lakes. The city of Joensuu itself was a minor place. With a population of less than 50,000, it offered little cosmopolitan life to attract students and staff, not to be compared to the limited delights found in Tampere, Jyväskylä, or Oulu, let alone Turku and Helsinki. Notably, powerful groups in government and the old universities argued against the spread of research in the new ones then being distributed throughout the country. Resources would be better used if concentrated in just two or three places: "It has often been argued by the representatives of the older universities, such as Helsinki and Turku, that the new universities represent a serious drain on resources and thus are ultimately harmful to Finnish science and scholarship." (Kivinen and Rinne, 1991, p. 60) Just how many full-bodied research universities of different sizes would a nation of five million need and be willing to support?

Even within its own region, Joensuu was not free to develop certain important subjects and powerful faculties. Regional politics, played out in the national legislature, dictated that higher education in eastern Finland would be divided among three competing cities: Kuopio got medicine; Lappeenranta got technology; and Joensuu, with teacher education as its main task, was to have the "human sciences." If Finland were to develop a two-tier system during the 1970s and 1980s, consisting of a few major research universities located in the old cities and of minor regional places concentrating on first-degree instruction, Joensuu would clearly be situated in the bottom reaches of the lower tier. In the earliest national thinking about the university in the mid-1960s, as expressed in the 1966 Act founding it, there was "no mention of scientific research as there had been in the statutes of all the other universities. It looked as if the University of Joensuu was about to become the first Finnish regional university, or vocational university, with teaching only at undergraduate level, with no postgraduate education, and with no resources for academic research." (Pulliainen, 1987, p. 4)

Founded on teacher education, small in size, regionally oriented, and possibly denied resources for research, Joensuu faced the likelihood of a marginal role. But the constraining conditions and attitudes did not prevail. Steady academic drift toward a university profile of subjects became the first undertow of change. The intended "academizing" of teacher education generated growth of subject departments, initially in fields taught in secondary education in which teachers needed preparation, and then in other university subjects. Typically, the creation of a department went hand-in-hand with the appointment of a professor or associate professor. First year appointments made in mathematics, biology, and Finnish as well as in education (1969) were soon followed by appointments in such school-related subjects as history, physics, and geography (1970), literature and chemistry (1972), and psychology and English (1973). A turning point came at the end of the first decade (1979), with an appointment in a nonschool subject: a professorial chair was established in economics. In the first half of the 1980s, professorships in such nonschool fields as forestry and computer science were added. Departmentalism was on the march, to the point where in the mid-1980s the university grouped the growing number of chairs and departments in five university-type faculties: science, social sciences, humanities, education, and forestry.

Research was not left out. Joensuu's first major rector, Heikki Kirkinen (1971–1981), argued from the outset that research had to be included. An internationally renowned expert in Karelian history, previously on the Sorbonne faculty, he was able early in his term to establish a Karelian Research Institute charged with the task of carrying out research on Karelian culture, a broad mandate that could include the social sciences and such specialties as ecology. (Pulliainen, 1987, p. 4) The institute was seen by the rector and others at the new university as "a door to research." Money at the outset came from local supporters: national governmental agencies contributed later. The rector's wishes were also supported by the local leadership of the province who wanted above all to see the development of a strong multidimensional university that could help propel regional economic development and enhance local culture. And the new academics at the university had no intention of staying out of research. When for example a new professor, fresh out of Helsinki, came in 1973 to take up a chair in psychology, he brought a small research team with him. From the beginning he knew he would be doing research on life cycles and occupational choice which required long-term funding in order to follow cohorts over several decades. When forestry was added as a possible major sector of the young university in the early 1980s, the die was cast for all to see: faculty research would underpin teaching and study.

Thus in the first 15 years of its existence, between 1969 and the early 1980s,

Joensuu worked its way into the growing family of multifaculty Finnish universities (the two that had existed before the 1960s had become ten). The institution could not be mistaken for an enterprise limited to teacher training. Although education remained important, it had become but one faculty among five and was increasingly outweighed by staff in the sciences, social sciences, and humanities. But if the university had grown beyond its original highly limited intent, the insistent question of where it would stand as a Finnish, Scandinavian, and European university remained. Operating with two to three thousand students and just 20 to 25 chaired professors, it could not be truly comprehensive. Significant fields were left out or only lightly staffed; departments that might want to cover five specialties could at best only effectively staff one or two. At the table of Finnish universities, Joensuu seemed destined to sit well down past the salt.

The institution's next major rector, Kyösti Pulliainen (1984–1990), felt upon taking office that "Joensuu was a weak university." Lacking the stability of tradition and subject to the vagaries of top-down control in a highly centralized national system, what would protect such a small, partial university if cutbacks in the national budget were enacted? Could the university even depend on equitable distribution of budget cuts – fair shares on the downslope – when more powerful universities could insist on protecting established "centers of excellence" – the "steeples" of the national system – at the cost, "regretfully" they would say, of slashing away at the margins? Even before the collapse of Finland's major trading partner, the USSR, those close to state finance could sense that the day would come in Finland when a large welfare-state public sector, including the universities, would be cut. There was ample reason to think that government would perceive higher education as particularly overextended. Regionalization had splashed universities of various sizes and shapes all over the country, even as far north as Rovaniemi near the Arctic Circle. Seventeen institutions were counted as universities (in a country of only five million people!), ten as multifaculty and seven as specialized, three each in the fields of economics and technology and one in veterinary medicine. (Kivinen and Rinne, 1991, p. 52) Situated in this extended university family, and facing a government about to change its ways, was there anything the university could do, other than wait and see? Could any major steps be taken to strengthen the institution?

The 1985–1995 Transformation

Among the five institutions analyzed in this study, Joensuu had the latest start as a university and was also relatively delayed in moving into a major entrepreneurial stage of development. Its critical actions did not fall into place until toward the end of the 1980s: hence it was even more of a work-in-progress in the mid-1990s than the other four institutions. But what was done in the space of six to eight years points to the value of foresight that led to vigorous steps.

Foresight at Joensuu took the form of recognizing that not only was the Finnish public sector heading toward major cost cutting but that in response to general budgetary constraints the national government would push its various sector agencies, long fixed in a tightly centralized mold, toward more independence. Less state, more market was seen to be in the offing. This recognition became the basis at the university for an *administrative thrust* that set in motion a new *institutional idea* centered on major *budgetary change* – a close fusing of three transforming elements.

On strengthening the *administration core*: Kyösti Pulliainen had been professor of economics, head of his department, head of the Karelian Institute, and first dean of social sciences, when he took up the rectorship in 1984, to serve, it turned out, for two three-year terms. The drift in Finnish public administration was identified by him and a small group of central administrators – the director of administration, the head of personnel and finance – as a "chance to exploit" the new willingness in government to decentralize from state to university. The Joensuu administrators proposed and obtained approval from the minister of education for the university to become "a pilot institution," one that would experiment for the system at large in "lump-sum budgeting." After two-to-three years of such experimentation, this major step in decentralization would then be spread, if possible, to all universities: they all would then replace segmented national allocations that came equipped with regulations on all conceivable expenditures with a single lump-sum allocation each university could largely spend as it wished; monies could then be moved across what had previously been water-tight categories. This new system even promised that funds not spent in the current year could be kept as local savings and carried over to the next year, eliminating the embedded bureaucratic irrationality that funds not spent within the current fiscal year had to be turned back to the government, a requirement that made the last month of the fiscal year throughout government in Finland and elsewhere into a free-for-all for spending.

To the notion of decentralizing control from state to university by means of a global budget, Joensuu added the radical idea of decentralizing internally by lump-sum allocation to departments and other basic units. The first step was readily acceptable to academics. Who did not want the greater institutional autonomy gained when government stepped back from detailed control and left the money, in effect, "on the stump"? But the second was a more delicate matter. For faculty and administrators alike, it tore up traditional lines of basic-unit income and expenditure, thereby trampling on old securities. The experience in Finland, as in other countries with such budgeting, soon showed that faculty can be quite unsure at the outset whether they want such full responsibility for deciding on *how* money will be spent within their domain, particularly on *who* will decide – a strengthened department head, the full professors within their separate internal domains, an elected council, or an inclusive department body of faculty, students, and nonacademic staff. And always lurking in faculty circles are doubts about "management": what's in it for the administration? Do "they" really mean it? Is there a hidden administrative hand in all this?

In practice at Joensuu, the idea of decentralized budgetary control was implemented through a series of incremental steps. Monies traditionally apportioned directly to such major service units as the library and computer centers were switched over, in large part, to faculties and departments: they would decide what library and computer service they would need and then pay for. The departments liked that. Some earmarked segments in the old budgets were lumped together. Departments also favored that. Two outsiders, Eila Rekilä and Seppo Hölttä, were employed to assist the rector in implementation. Rekilä had been senior planning official in the Ministry of Education and was hired for two years to work at Joensuu on the budgetary reform. Her participation in the reform helped to convince central ministers to approve the experiment. Offering a different backgound, Hölttä had earlier studied in the United States with Howard Bowen at the Claremont Graduate School and with me at the UCLA Graduate School of Education. He knew the international literature in the economics and organizational analysis of higher education. Fresh to the organization and able to work with departments on problems of switching over to the new system, their work gave additional credence to the promise that all departments could learn to handle lump-sum budgeting and profit from it. Matti Halonen, who had been with the university from the day it opened, provided reassuring stability as director of administration even as he served as the closest collaborator for rectors deeply engaged in reform. In the late 1980s, all practices were trial and error; across-the-board application was effected in 1990.

The overall team assembled by Pulliainen to push through this reform consisted largely of central staff: rector, administrative director, finance director, head of study affairs, and the two new planning officers. When faculty reluctance to go along with the reform was voiced in senate resistance to the rector's leadership, the time had come "to separate the reform from the person." A new rector, Paavo Pelkonen, who had come to the university in the early 1980s to develop the Faculty of Forestry and later served as dean of faculty, was elected in 1990. Committed to the reform, Pelkonen changed the central steering group to include more elected faculty. In an "experimental leading group" the rector and administrative director met periodically with two elected vice-rectors and three faculty drawn from the ranks of department heads to deliberate "strategic questions." For operational work the rector and director then met as often as needed with other members of the administrative staff. The hard push of the 1985–1990 years to get the reform started became a sustained effort to elicit faculty cooperation in spreading the reform throughout the basic units. Managerial adjustments continued in the early and mid-1990s. When the concept of a leading group comprised largely of "regular faculty members" proved insufficient, the role of deans was strengthened. Since they were more comprehensively informed about the situation in various departments, especially as affected by budget decreases, the rector turned to them as links to the basic units.

As the Joensuu experiment continued the departments gradually learned how to manage their individual lump-sum budgets. But as elsewhere, some of them developed such capability much more quickly and fully than did others. Science departments were in the forefront of change. Involvement in research grants and industrial contracts had taught them how to handle relatively large sums of money from multiple sources. Research groups were accustomed to raising and spending a certain amount of money on their own, offering the possibility that a science department could in turn immediately allocate lump-sums to several research groups located within it. Other departments were not so well situated to sense that advantages could outweigh disadvantages. Humanities and social science departments and the faculty of education, by and large, had not worked with large sums of money raised outside of fixed, national budgetary lines. They had not typically pursued a steady stream of research grants from research councils of the Academy of Finland or from industry, noneducation ministries, and transnational European bodies. They had not been as much involved in using temporary personnel supported by "temporary funds." Mainline institutional support from a single national source was their base of security. It was also a basis for a passive departmental outlook. The essentials of salary and rank for faculty, and support for students, were given. Allocations changed annually by state-set increments. Staff could then get on with their teaching and research without taking on the onerous responsibility of balancing one expenditure against another and thereby directly facing the harsh reality that every benefit has a cost, that money spent on one item was money that could not be spent on alternative uses.

During the early 1990s the Joensuu administration and faculty worked out the kinks in the processes of lump-sum budgeting to departments and faculty acceptance became widespread. The *idea* of budgetary-based self-regulation worked its way into operational practice, spreading from the administrative core into the *academic heartland*. The Joensuu credo became simple: if departments are "basic units" they should be budget-holders. They should be given as much leeway as possible to develop their disciplinary possibilities. Beginning in 1990, this decentralization idea was given theoretical support by reference to cross-national literature on higher education in which the disciplinary-institutional matrix structure of universities and their heavy structuring around disciplinary cultures had been highlighted. (Clark, 1983; Becher and Kogan, 1980, 1992; Brennan, 1986; Becher, 1989; Van Vught, 1989) Officials could then claim that Joensuu was carrying "theory to practice."

The reasoning of Joensuu administrators was highly instructive. They pointed to the need to begin always with the special nature of higher education organizations. What should be the guiding principles for the management of reform?

> The university did not want to accept the standard management models applied to other public organizations in Finland. Instead, a solution was sought by studying the special features of academic organization and academic work. (Höltta and Pulliainen, 1992, p. 2)

What were those special features?

> The disciplinary organizations are exceptionally independent; they are the sources of values and norms for academic work and are characterized by self-control. (p. 55)

What then followed for management-led reform?

> The central question in developing new kinds of management models is how the administrative system and management methods would be able most effectively to support academic activities. In practice, no other conclusion than internal decentralization of universities and strengthening of disciplines could be directly drawn from the theoretical analysis. (p. 55)

Root-and-branch decentralization was thus seen as the first requirement. But it would immediately require new administrative integrative devices:

> The project group also saw the problems in this kind of decentralized development: the university needs leadership, strategies and goals, which are shared by disciplines and departments. Integrating elements have to be built into the new management system also from the point of view of public accountability. (p. 55)

Turning departments loose by giving them budgetary self-control thus turned out to be only half of the equation of change. In Finland or anywhere else, this step alone would simply set in motion centrifugal forces of departmental aggrandizement that would fracture the university into disparate parts flying off in different directions. What would be left could not even be dignified as a confederation. New countervailing forces would have to be brought into play, new ways of uniting the departments and asserting the broader institutional interest. Those ways at Joensuu soon marched primarily under two headings: "dialogue" and "information systems." Each contribute to a *strengthened administrative core*.

"Dialogue," in practice, came to mean that the rector and one or two immediate colleagues (administrative director, a planning officer) would make the rounds of the departments periodically, once or twice a year, to discuss departmental plans, achievements, and problems. In a system much in flux, a visit might be made to a faculty as a whole, but in a small university committed to "short lines" and "flat structure," the conversation was usually between rector's office and department. The Joensuu version of "dialogue" stressed informal relations and transparent exchange of information. But whatever the softness of the means, the gaze of the center was brought to bear on what the department was and was not doing. In effect, the university as a whole walked into the department and looked around.

"Information systems," evolving year by year, meant that the administrative center of the university has had increasingly integrated measures on each department. With modern computers, separate sets of data on student admission, student completion, faculty salary, faculty work load, support staff, premises, library, and research funding could be put together and related to one another, both for departmental and central use. (Halonen, Hölttä, and Pulliainen, 1993) Departments can then be compared on sources of support, unit costs, and such "outputs" as degree completion, faculty course coverage, and faculty research productivity. As the government and the universities agreed on what information should go forward to the Ministry of Education, some of the above data systems also hooked into "a national data base (KOTA)" that presented comparable data on all universities, especially on resources and "outputs." "Information systems" are no idle matter, affecting the autonomy of departments and universities and the assessment of one organizational level by another.

In the mid-1990s the central officers of the university were much preoccupied with the issue of how best to assert "the institutional interest." As planned, power had indeed gone off to the departments. But the counterbalancing force of central integration, and especially central initiative, was problematic. How should the center, and possibly the faculties, vis-à-vis the departments, be strengthened so that the university and its major components could decide on certain foci and shift resources accordingly? Many impediments blocked easy solutions. The normal vested interests of disciplinarians in protecting and furthering the development of their "own" territory was deepened at Joensuu by the combination of small size and professorial chairs in which the loss of a senior member, primarily through retirement, could threaten the very existence of a department. This sharply limited the likelihood of vacancies reverting to the center for cross-department reallocation. "Short lines" also meant that the faculty level could not be depended on for much flexible reallocation: if the departments were the major "budget-holders," then the five faculties were not. The structure put considerable pressure on the rector and his immediate colleagues to assert overall direction. One effective line of influence came through the maintenance of monies at the center as "strategic funds," amounting to about seven percent of total budget, from which selective investments in fields could be made. Physics was so favored, as we see later, where a major commitment in personnel and equipment in the specialty of optics was made.

Beyond the lump-sum budgeting experiment, Joensuu also moved into a second major reform known as "flexible work load." This reform was piloted at the University of Jyväskylä and the Helsinki School of Economics and Business Administration, beginning in 1988. Joensuu adapted it in 1992: as of early 1996, these three institutions, out of 17 universities, were the only ones willing or able to do so (national unions have resisted its spread beyond the three). Joensuu faculty soon came to see this second line of reform as complementary to lump-sum budgeting. The idea was simple: within a nationally set workload requirement of 1600 hours each academic year, faculty could negotiate with their department heads on allocation of their time between four major tasks of education, research, public services, and other responsibilities. They could change the mix from year to year, particularly to favor more research in one year (or part of a year) and more teaching in another. (Höltta and Karjalainen, 1997)

Such flexibility may not be new to academics in some other national systems who have the autonomy to change their own teaching assignments, research engagements, and committee work from year to year largely as they pleased, with no national guidelines and only light departmental supervision. But in Finland a highly centralized mold, including national union contracts, meant that rigid teaching loads were nationally, and then institutionally, specified by personnel categories of professor, associate professor, lecturer, senior assistant, assistant, and part-time teachers. (Höltta and Nuotio, 1995) The flexible workload scheme threw all that out: departments could now allocate faculty time as they pleased; they could also buy services from outside, for example, from local clinical psychologists for the psychology department. Research on this system at Joensuu in 1995 reported that faculty did not want to return "to the old rigid teaching hours," even if the new system did not fulfill all initial promises. Lack of resources was still an underlying constraint: in a time of budget cuts, the imperatives of staffing department courses loomed large. But some flexibility had clearly been gained, including time for reconstructing courses as well as for periods of intense research activity. Teachers felt freer to replace lectures by group work, examinations by reports. (Höltta and Karjalainen, 1997) "Flexible work load" added another dimension to "lump-sum budgeting" in enhancing departmental discretion.

This double reform changed departmental administration and behavior throughout the university. As responsibility became localized, and discretionary money developed, departments and the central leadership had motive and opportunity to think more sharply about how to build departments into recognized "centers of excellence," to raise units as "steeples" in the institutional profile. Several scientific fields were particularly motivated and positioned to garner the extra resources that would permit them to move ahead. Especially in chemistry and physics, and then in the special professional field of forestry, entrepreneurial action became strongly evident in *the academic heartland.*

Chemistry was brought into the university in 1972, shortly after it opened, as a subject in which to prepare school teachers. By the early 1980s the department strongly emphasized research and defined itself as a significant part of the effort "to build a research university." A future important department head, Tapani Pakkanen, was actively building a research group that by the mid-1990s had grown to 20 staff, including graduate students. One senior professor in the department became two, two became five professors and associate professors heading up research groups. Undergraduate students majoring in chemistry on "teacher education lines" were soon greatly outnumbered by students on "general study lines" – by 1994, 36 compared to 145. (University of Joensuu, 1994b, p. 4) As the department increasingly stressed its research base, its funding diversified: monies were obtained not only from the research council line – councils within the Academy of Finland – but also from noneducation ministries, a new national Technology Development Center (TEKES), private industry, and special funding from the university. Dependence on mainline ministerial support, "basic university funding," dropped by the mid-1990s to one-half of departmental income.

Lump-sum budgeting fitted this highly active unit so well that the department took the procedure an extra step, dividing its budget into separate sums to be allocated to four internal research groups, an action that defines an additional dimension in just how far modern universities can go in decentralizing budgetary authority. Since each laboratory group ran its own budget, the chair of the department could then just track a few indicators and otherwise treat the group's self-steerage as a "black box." The chair's internal administrative duties then amounted to just a few hours each week, a remarkable outcome in a day of increasingly overworked department heads.

The chemistry department at Joensuu also worked hard to devise an attractive program for first-degree students. Students in Finland can freely apply to as many universities as they wish. As in Germany, they are deemed to be adults ready to specialize: they apply to departments and are accepted by them (via formal faculty decision). The Joensuu chemistry department had had a low "yield" of acceptance from its offers: among six chemistry departments in Finland, Joensuu was "at the bottom" in the attractiveness of "city beautiful." Viewing its 30 percent yield as unacceptable, the department adopted the strategy of a small special program made highly selective by personally interviewing all applicants and selecting only a small number, 15 or so, at the outset. Other students were also culled during the first year, with rejects allowed to move to other disciplines. Students in the selective cohorts were soon admitted to research groups in the department. They were also allowed to skip some first-year courses, they were employed in the summer, they were promised that they could complete their first-degree in four rather than five or six years and otherwise made to feel "very special." As a new perception got around, the acceptance-to-offer ratio went up to 80 percent. By such means, the department increasingly produced graduates who were highly motivated and wanted to continue. Over one-half went directly on to doctoral study in the same department, propelled on their way by the undergraduate work. Student involvement was clearly taken as critical. In contrast to the trend elsewhere for intense laboratory-based teaching and learning to lose out in undergraduate "mass" instruction and to shift entirely to the advanced levels, the department's laboratory groups involved undergraduate as well as graduate students.

An international evaluation committee, commissioned by the university to evaluate the Faculty of Science and staffed by experts from six countries, praised the chemistry department in a 1993 report as one operating "at an outstanding international level and its output is found in many of the most important journals of the field." Further: "the degree productivity of the department is also the highest in Finland [among chemistry departments] and so is the extremely high share of external funding, in particular industrial funding: both far above the national average." (University of Joensuu, 1993, p. 3) Departmental leadership was exceptional. In the mid-1990s highly regarded Professor Pakkanen served simultaneously as head of department and as head of one of the four research councils of the national academy, placing him two days a week, and more, in the midst of the Helsinki crossroads of Finnish science. Occupying administrative roles that at their best were heavily time consuming, Pakkanen faced the problem of responsible leading scientists: "Either I stop doing administration or I stop doing science."

Physics is a second field in which the university has chosen to allocate scarce resources out of its limited discretionary funds. Even more sharply in this expensive field, hard choices had to be made for a small department in a small university. If a wide waterfront of specialty coverage could not even be considered, what one or two foci in physics could possibly be developed? Optics was an early, fortunate choice; it was started in the 1980s, and pushed hard, relative to the rest of the university, in the 1990s. The international committee commissioned to review the work of the entire Faculty of Science commented in 1993 that "the original selection of Optics as a field of specialization has been a wise choice for a relatively small department." (University of Joensuu, 1993, p. 4) Four research groups that came together in the general area of "information optics and optical materials" made the department "the most important optics research centre in Finland." (University of Joensuu, 1994b, p. 9) Professors in the department saw the optics specialty as a close fusing of "basic" and "applied," a focus that allows them to make basic contributions to the international literature while also engaged in industrial application. They also have an ongoing collaboration with research institutes in Germany, France, Switzerland, Russia, and Japan, which minimizes the isolation of their Karelian location.

Starting in 1993 the physics department has benefited from the strong, determined leadership of Timo Jääskeläinen as a department head who had both extended international ties, particularly with Japanese researchers, and major research reputation. Like chemistry, the physics department has been gradually diversifying its sources of support – industry, European Union, Academy of Finland, other government agencies – dropping its dependence on mainline support below 50 percent. In 1996 the department was heading into a large project funded by the EU that was "more than our regular budget." Helped by the Technology Development Center of Finland in securing such joint European projects – applied and collaborative – the department felt that such projects "guarantee more money and are easier to get" than grants from the Finnish Academy. Also starting up, with fast implementation of plans, was a "clean room" laboratory that could bring in big projects from throughout Europe as well as from Finnish companies. Here seemed "an opportunity at the forefront," a facility at Joensuu that would have both major promise for basic findings and offer critical aid to industrial companies without such equipment of their own. If the University of California, San Diego could be observed running a somewhat similar laboratory in the mid-1990s, reportedly with user charges of $400 per hour, why couldn't Joensuu operate its clean room in a similar fashion? With user time limited by technical requirements to no more than twelve hours a day, perhaps ten hours could be allocated for staff research and several hours for income purposes. Why so many more hours for the department's own research? "Because this is a university, not a company." The specialty of optics and a related clean room laboratory are vivid examples of choice of focus. For the department, the university, and the Finnish scientific community, the choice entails a major opportunity, and major risk, in a concentrated investment of limited resources.

Physics and chemistry, organizational steeples in the academic heartland of Joensuu, are able to claim flexibility in the way they have organized their efforts. They assert first that flexibility can be seen as a general advantage of small universities, especially in European public-university frameworks: "Joensuu is much more flexible than Helsinki." The first had "short lines," where senior faculty can relate directly to the rector, while the latter was seen as clogged with rigid hierarchies and related bureaucratic rules. Second, flexibility is seen as enhanced by organizing research groups within departments instead of in separate research institutes that acquire an organizational life of their own. And finally, only some personnel in the department need be seen as full-time and permanent – half or less – while the rest, including graduate students defined as research workers, are temporary and serve in posts that vary from one to five years. They then move on, hopefully well-prepared by their training and experience to gain good positions elsewhere, outside or within the academy.

Since personnel costs loom large in university budgets, the lesson is pointed. Flexibility, an increasingly desirable characteristic in universities, means that "temporary money" can support only "temporary people," especially in departments that keep their own ledgers under lump-sum budgeting. Entire universities or major segments thereof may possibly support some permanent staff on a rolling portfolio of "soft" income streams. But this possibility is drastically reduced at the department level, especially when small and highly focused. Then temporary money must mean temporary personnel. Employment less than permanent, and often less than full-time, is the trade-off if departments are to flexibly adjust from one year to the next, one set of projects to another.

Forestry is a third field that plays a distinctive role in the outreach and entrepreneurial actions of the University of Joensuu. The field has a fascinating resonance in Finnish culture as well as connections to a basic industry.

With 70 percent of the country covered by forests, Finns have an age-old traditional love of their wooded rural areas. Finnish architecture, arts, and crafts based on imaginative use of wood lead even the most cosmopolitan sectors of the population to connect forestry products to national identity. In 1996, declared the National Year of Wood, the Museum of Finnish Architecture in Helsinki appropriately claimed that "wood is a familiar, close and natural material for every Finn. In our old peasant culture, almost everything needed for everyday life was made of wood [and] timber is still one of the basic materials of Finnish architecture, design and art." Beyond that, "wood is an ecological and renewable natural resource of unbelievably diverse properties," even "a warm material with soul." No wonder then that "today, wood is more timely and topical than ever." (Museum of Finnish Architecture, 1996)

The world of Finnish commerce had good reason to agree: the timber and wood-processing industry ranks as a primary sector of the national economy, still able to rival in the mid-1990s the economic importance of the metal industry and that new upstart, "high tech." Viewing itself in the nineties as a "high-tech" country, Finland has used the new to bolster the old. In the view of the government: "Even more important than direct [high technology] exports is the fact that continuous interaction with indigenous high-tech research, development and industry keeps the still-vital Finnish wood-processing and forest industries competitive." (Ministry of Education, 1994a, p. 27) Direct high technology exports, although of rapidly growing importance, were still only about 15 percent of total exports in 1992. Forestry products, down from the 70 percent of 1960, were still about 37 percent. High-tech innovations were used to improve the metal and electronics industry that produced the machinery for the work of the timber industry. The government saw "profitable niches for innovative high-tech industry" in its interaction with a traditional basic one, forestry. (pp. 27–28)

With forestry so important culturally and commercially, Finland has long paid close attention to its development. Through decades of cooperation between public agencies, commercial firms, and private farms, Finland by the 1990s arrived at a "sustainable forest"; it grew more trees than were cut down, a feat of pride for any nation. On a continuum of forest sustainability, it stood along with Sweden as the very opposite of Brazil and Indonesia. Other nations in Europe as well as on other continents, deeply concerned about the depletion of this important natural resource, have shown interest in what the Finns do. A strong research effort has followed. In total number of forest researchers, small Finland was only behind Germany, France, and Sweden in Western Europe; in the share of such researchers among all of a country's scientists, it stood first. (The Finnish Society of Forest Science, 1995, p. 15)

After the usual resistance of the University of Helsinki – the seat of Finland's traditional forestry faculty – on grounds of diffusion of resources and unnecessary duplication, a study program for a first degree (master's level) in forestry was introduced at Joensuu in 1981. The field became a full-blown faculty when the university went to a structure of five major units in the mid-1980s. A decade later the faculty had grown to a staff of 100, including 10 senior professors, and a student body of 60 advanced students and 200 undergraduates. Committed to research on "the boreal forest ecosystem, Finland's principal natural resource," the faculty aims to train "forest ecology researchers" as well as foresters able to engage in the broad management of forests, forest technology, and the wood industry in different parts of the world, equipped with "the principles of sustainable development." (University of Joensuu, 1995, 1996) The faculty's revenue from external funding exceeded its income from the basic institutional line: in 1995, 12 million Finnish marks from outside sources compared to 8 million from the Ministry of Education. External sources included the European Union, industry, the Finnish Academy of Science, and a noneducation bureau, the Finnish Ministry of Agriculture and Forestry.

The forestry faculty has received scientific praise and support for its work. In 1994 the Academy of Finland, in a highly competitive process reaching across all universities and disciplines, designated 12 national centers of excellence as a way to promote high-quality university research. Seven of the new centers were located in Helsinki, two were based in Turku, and just three were found in all the other university locations: one in Tampere, in the southern part of the country, one off in Oulu in western Finland, and one at Joensuu, under Seppo Kellomaki, in forestry, specifically on "response of the boreal forest ecosystem to climatic change" and how the management of that system "should be adjusted in order to maintain sustainable forest yield." (Ministry of Education, 1994b, p. 15) This major award from *the* science body of the country recognized research that had been underway since 1990 at the university as part of a broad Finnish effort to study the effects of climatic change. It testified to and furthered the growth of a high reputation for the Faculty of Forestry, insuring that it would be seen outside and inside the university as a steeple.

At the same time the faculty became a strong basic unit in the academic heartland it also took up a central role in the institution's *developmental periphery*. It has systematic outreach not only in its own direct relations to industry and outside professional bodies but also through its ties to two research institutes, one located on campus and one nearby in the city, that help make urban Joensuu a place where theory and practice in forestry are closely connected. A Forest Research Station, one of eight in the country, was established in the city the same year that the study of forestry was initiated at the university. Although operating under the Ministry of Agriculture and Forestry, not the education ministry, the Research Station has worked so closely with the Faculty of Forestry that, in the mid-1990s, the two took up joint residence in a new university building and shared laboratory space. The station's full- and part-time personnel have grown to about 100. (Finnish Forest

Research Institute, 1996) The university-research station structure is similar to the historic outreach of American land-grant universities to practitioners by means of agricultural research stations. The faculty and the station are seen as having "different cultures," the one more academic, led by Ph.D. staff, the other more practical, more field involved, with largely a non-Ph.D. staff.

The second related enterprise is the European Forest Institute (EFI), supported by both European bodies and the Finnish government. It is committed to serving Europe especially with "problem-oriented analysis" that stretches from forest sustainability to changes in markets for forest products to forest sector information services (European Forest Institute, 1995). The "know-how" of the university's forestry faculty was a key consideration in locating the institute in the city of Joensuu against the wishes of many other Finnish towns that wanted it. With his expertise in forestry, the rector of the university, Paavo Pelkonen, was particularly helpful in getting the institute started. EFI considers itself nongovernmental, supported by private sources, the EU, multiple national governments, and fees from 60 institutional members located in over 30 countries. Its conferences bring experts from other countries to the Joensuu headquarters; faculty members from the university are involved. With about 150 and more researchers located together in the university and in the two outreach institutes, Joensuu became a major European site.

More plans were afoot. The forestry complex was undergoing further development in the mid-1990s: an Institute of Forestry and Wood Technology within a newly assembled North Karelian Polytechnic was established. The new polytechnic sector of Finnish higher education – the AMK sector (ammattikorkeakoulu in Finnish) – only initiated in 1991, involves upgrading an old vocational education system. The new polys will "offer three-to-four-year courses giving qualifications comparable to university degrees but with more of an occupational emphasis." (Organisation for Economic Co-operation and Development (OECD), 1995, p. 95) This local polytechnic soon forged new agreements on cooperation with the university in research, teaching, and shared services, for example, library and information services. Its emphasis on "practical studies" means "hands on" forestry training close to practice. (North Karelia Polytechnic, 1996) As the poly develops, the university forestry faculty will all the more sit as the scholarly anchor in a local complex of organizations that systematically reaches to practitioners in this basic, dispersed industry.

Forestry has become a major focus in the university to the point where social scientists concerned about the relatively weak position of their disciplines even look to the possibility of becoming linked to it through environmental studies, economic analysis, and social policy. Others sense that biology can be strengthened by linking it more closely to forestry. And with just two main national locations for university teaching in forestry, the Joensuu faculty cannot miss having a significant national profile, with some advantages of organization and location. At the University of Helsinki, work in forestry has been diffused among some three dedicated and four related departments within a large Faculty of Agriculture and Forestry, which in turn is located within a huge fully comprehensive university of 33,000 students, five times the size of Joensuu. Joensuu has a highly integrated faculty, one not divided into departments, in a much smaller university. It is also located out where forests abound rather than in the confines of the country's largest city.

Developments in the sciences and forestry have placed these fields at the cutting edge of the university's overall move into more *diversified funding*. The university in 1980 was completely dependent on its governmental core support, at 96 percent. That fiscal dependence dropped 30 percentage points in 15 years, to 66 percent in 1995. The second income stream, research councils, increased from 1 to a-still-low 7 percent; the third stream was the one that became highly significant, increasing from 3 to 27 percent (see table 6–1). The later university overall figure was tugged upward particularly by forestry, which in 1995 was receiving three-fifths of its income from other than its basic governmental support. The science departments were all tending in this direction, led by chemistry and physics with half of income from noncore allocation.

TABLE 6–1

Sources of Financial Support, University of Joensuu, 1980–1995
(millions of Finnish marks)

Year	Core Support Amount	Core Support Percent	Research Councils Amount	Research Councils Percent	All Other Sources Amount	All Other Sources Percent	Total Amount	Total Percent
1980	28.3	96	0.4	1	0.9	3	29.6	100
1985	72.5	94	1.8	2	2.7	4	77.0	100
1990	88.3	70	6.5	5	31.7	25	126.5	100
1995	155.0*	66	15.7	7	63.6	27	234.3	100

*Total government outlay of 222.7 million included two new allocations not previously included: 45 million for the university to pay rent on its buildings; and 22 million to make payments on a retirement fund. The comparable figure then becomes approximately 155 million. *Source*: income trend data compiled by Seppo Höltta, Director of Planning and Development, University of Joensuu

As mentioned earlier, the faculties of social sciences, humanities, and education have been less involved in relationships that link with outside groups and produce income than the faculties of science and forestry. A relatively weak social science faculty has sought to move toward social policy interests; psychology is positioned to move further into the broad world of vocational counseling. Humanities makes its way on extended undergraduate interest in history, cultural studies, and languages; these subjects draw core support based on student numbers. And the faculty of education, deeply involved in teacher education for eastern Finland, has continued to be a major segment of the institution. In 1993 it had slightly over 30 percent of the students and of the faculty, and conferred one-half of all degrees. But many faculty members were lecturers and part-time teachers: the faculty had less than 20 percent of senior rank faculty and less than 20 percent of the university budget. (University of Joensuu, 1994a, Appendix 3) Its possibilities of raising external funds seem to lie in development projects for developing societies and in the work of a Research and Development Center for Information Technology in Education newly energized in the mid-1990s. Professors in other faculties, especially science, felt that "the education faculty is off by itself." In academic centrality, the faculties of humanities and social sciences were positioned somewhat between forestry and the sciences on the one side and education on the other.

How can the humanities reach out from their traditional departmental locations to become, even in a minor way, participants in a university's developmental periphery? Could their personnel even be found in a science park? Sometimes students show us the way. At Joensuu in 1993 three undergraduate students in folklore studies, intensely interested in computers, decided they could work up a multimedia representation of pictures and text as a new way of presenting cultural heritage. They worked for three years gathering and integrating 1,000 photographs on the Kalevala, the classic epic poem of Finland born from the oral tradition of the Karelia region. After much hard work – a labor of love, with minor financial support – they and a handful of friends produced in early 1996 a CD-Rom titled "Hyper Kalevala." On the way to the finished product, they organized a small company – "we just figured it out" – and marketed the disk through a publisher. "Hyper Kalevala" depicts Finnish folk culture from the earlier rock paintings to 20th century art; it stresses cultural continuity from oral to written traditions stretching over many centuries. The final product has caught public attention and the possibility of royalties. It can be used in the schools, in all grade levels, including higher and adult education. It was a model, apparently the first of its kind in Finland, of what could be done with historical materials and old photographs in multimedia form. With the huge potential for "presenting pictures," the possibilities seem endless. The final product is easy to use but hard to make, involving much tedious work and substantial front-end costs.

The student – 30 years old – interviewed about this remarkable project had gone on to graduate work in cultural studies at the university. Under stipend as a research worker, he was attempting to arrange "in scientific form" the materials from "Hyper Kalevala." Although a graduate student in the humanities, he held down an office in a multimedia section of the Karelian Science Park.

The university has been a late-comer in efforts to develop a science park as a major part of its developmental periphery. Forestry had its own means of outreach; chemistry, physics, and the other science departments similarly were able to reach out to industry and other external sectors from their university bases. The university did not have engineering, a field basic to science park development at most universities and one that played a key role in the build-up of a major park, Oulu Technopolis, with Nokia as anchor tenant, near the

University of Oulu. Also, the city of Joensuu has not been seen as a major center of industry, nor as a particularly favorable location for new high-tech enterprises, compared to, for example, the Helsinki region, Turku, and Oulu. But starting in 1990, a science-park effort has been undertaken in which the university plays a key role. The Karelian Science Park, organized legally as a separate corporation, moved into new premises in 1994, close to the university. With three-way support from the city, the region, and the university, it is prepared to rent space to companies, offer a training course for entrepreneurs, and assist in promoting technology transfer. With 40 companies but only three times that number of persons, the park sees itself as a place for small spin-off firms. Part of a nationwide network of over a dozen technology parks, it participates in Finland's Innovation Relay Centre enterprise, a network tied into a much larger all-Europe complex that assists firms and institutions wanting to buy or sell technology. University involvement in the park has been greatest in forestry, followed by physics (optics), and chemistry (chemical technology). Unfortunately, for purposes of income generation, patents are held in Finland by individual investors. Hence, no money was in the offing for the park or university from intellectual property rights.

*   *   *   *

We close the analysis with a revealing picture of the differences in "degree production" that have developed among the five faculties of the university. The science faculty produces only 15 percent of first degrees and then jumps to 46 percent of Ph.Ds. Forestry follows suit, from 7 to 18 percent. Together,

TABLE 6–2

Basic Degrees and Doctoral Degrees, University of Joensuu, by Faculty, 1995
University share (in percent)

Faculty	Basic degree		Doctoral Degree	
Science	15 ⎫	22	46 ⎫	64
Forestry	7 ⎭		18 ⎭	
Social Sciences	16		9	
Humanities	24 ⎫	62	15 ⎫	27
Education	38 ⎭		12 ⎭	
	100		100	

Source: Faculty of Science Annual Report 1995, University of Joensuu, pp. 4–5

science and forestry produce two-thirds of the doctorates. The other three faculties show the opposite pattern: they are important in the undergraduate realm, with humanities and education producing about two-thirds of the basic degrees, but have only a small role in doctoral work. Education contrasts sharply with science, dropping from 38 percent of first degrees to 12 percent of doctorates. Joensuu's investments in science and forestry to build larger research foundations in those fields has been a simultaneous investment in research training at the highest level in those fields. Performing a service role for the Karelia region, education and the humanities dominate the undergraduate realm.

Conclusion

At the end of a quarter-century of existence, the University of Joensuu had staked a claim in the Finnish system of higher education that was very different from the one offered it at the outset. In a first stage of development it negotiated passage from an all-encompassing emphasis on teacher education for the local region to a semicomprehensive array of university departments eager to do research and to engage in research-based teaching and learning. The institution was not going to be constrained by a tightly limited role; in effect it would not be kept "down on the farm" after it had seen the delights of the university big city. In a second stage characterized by locally instigated reform, work still in progress in the mid-1990s, the university asserted a capacity for self-development that moved it toward the character of an entrepreneurial university. It took the opportunity to serve as an experimental pilot institution in lump-sum budgeting from state to university. It then pushed that idea deeper, from university to operating units, thereby pressuring departments to assume active postures. Joensuu took seriously the credo that if basic units are basic they should have almost total control over individual global budgets. Such control would liberate disciplinary impulses. But with this strengthening of departmental control came the need to strengthen the capacity of the institution generally to hold together the centrifugal thrusts of the departments and institutes and to strengthen the means of all-university steerage. Stronger basic unit control generated a need for a permanently strengthened central staff and other new means of integration.

In the transformation of Joensuu, the five elements highlighted in our five-country analysis have been at work. A special administrative core has steadily emerged, combining managerial and academic points of view in a center-faculty-department organizational backbone. Authority has tended to become more vested in the positions of rector, faculty dean, and department head. At the same time faculty members have been brought into the university's "central groups," there to be made responsible for institutional rather than sectorial interests. New revenue streams have been added in a steady diversification of income: from top to bottom, funds obtained from other than governmental core support have enhanced discretion. A useful developmental periphery has been evolving, promoting a more organized and more diversified capacity to reach out across traditional university boundaries to a host of private and public outside agencies and populations. A set of institutional self-conceptions have gradually evolved in which self-regulation and entrepreneurial outlook predominate. The university pushes all its fields "to make business," at the least to engage in more continuing education. Departments are spurred to look to their income possibilities. The heartland of academic departments has increasingly exhibited entrepreneurial action, with the sciences and forestry out in front and the humanities and social sciences lagging somewhat behind as they struggled toward collective capacities to stand responsibly on their feet and reduce their dependence on shrinking governmental patronage.

Joensuu's road to transformation has been a difficult one. Its possibilities of outreach to a rapidly changing, complex environment have been sharply limited by its subject capabilities. It has not had engineering, or business, or medicine, fields that in other universities serve as leading salients of outreach. It has had to operate from the posture of a comprehensive university in which small size and regional role have dictated limited coverage, especially in the humanities and social sciences but also stretching across the increasingly expensive physical and biological sciences. Not only limited in the arts and sciences, the university has also been restricted to just two major "applied" or "professional" areas – education and forestry – from which to build new forms of outreach. Here, forestry has developed into a major point of competitive advantage.

As a young university, Joensuu has shown in its first quarter-century the advantages of newness. One highly regarded faculty member after another spoke in interview of the flexibility gained in their own research and teaching by taking a post at this remote place. Central officials spoke of the greater institutional flexibility of a newer *and* smaller place where the cake of custom had not hardened and informal relations could smooth the way. Similar sentiments could be found at Jyväskylä and Oulu and at other regional universities established in recent decades. The huge University of Helsinki, serving as the flagship of the national system, remained attractive on the many grounds of tradition, reputation, embedded resources, established capability, and city location. Other places could not touch it for "solemn rituals." But room to maneuver was not one of its virtues; institutional rigidities were more massive and difficult to overcome. Faculty members out in the regions are then heard referring to it as a plodding flagship, even a stodgy elephant. Small Joensuu could maneuver. It could seize the opportunity to be a "pilot" institution, offering itself up to the risks of experimentation. Where the old Finnish system offered "security" by means of established and monitored categories of budgeting and job rights, the new emerging system exemplified here by Joensuu was seen as offering flexibility in newly evolved capacities to enhance resources, develop new infrastructure, and assert entrepreneurial responsibility in traditional departments.

Joensuu's possibilities within the limits of its size, location, and coverage of subjects seemed increasingly to translate into a substantive differentiation between first-degree (undergraduate) and advanced degree (graduate or postgraduate) work. In the humanities, the social sciences, and especially in teacher preparation, students complete their study with the first major degree: these fields have large enrollments at this level. In the sciences, students go on for advanced degrees and science departments award relatively large numbers of them. By the mid-1990s, a transforming Joensuu joined the other four universities we have studied in exhibiting a strong thrust toward coupling new forms of organization and finance with research training beyond the first basic degree.

In observing the capabilities of departments and research groupings at Joensuu to adjust, we gain additional glimmerings beyond those found at Warwick, Twente, Strathclyde, and Chalmers about how modern universities that seek to transform themselves become learning organizations. The main operational units, however diverse their subjects, are thrust into medium- and long-term planning. They individually have to search for a profile of activities around which they can prosper. They become sharply conscious of the need to construct departmental as well as institutional niches in national and international domains. But at the same time their planning must be tentative; flexibility in long-term outlook is needed in each basic unit to adjust the subject profile and the occupied niche to unknown circumstances in a fast changing world that may lie only a few years down the road. One by one, the operating components have to go on learning how capabilities match up with a changing array of externally set possibilities. At Joensuu, as passivity gave way to self-regulation, the basic units have learned much about how to learn their way.

Part III

University Transformation

7

The Problem of University Transformation

We have seen five European universities in action, each transforming itself over a period of ten to 15 years by vigorous effort that can be characterized as entrepreneurial. Each university's development is itself a complex institutional story, one best told when embedded in contextual peculiarities and unique features of organizational character. When thus portrayed, the universities offer different histories, settings, and profiles. We then know Warwick in the English Midlands as a major research university only three decades old that faced down hard times in the 1980s and positioned itself to compete with the best universities in its own country and the world. We know Joensuu in rural Finland as a minor comprehensive university formed out of humble beginnings in the late 1960s that had to take risks and push hard 15 years later simply to achieve a sustainable niche in its own national system. As a completely technological university located on the west coast of Sweden we see Chalmers as a place that has retained a specialized form even as it asserts innovative strength across a spectrum of fields in engineering and applied science and assumes a special status in the Swedish university system. Twente, hard by the German border in The Netherlands, stands as a technological university of somewhat broader character, with a growing second focus in applied social science and its own set of distinctive campus features. Glasgow's Strathclyde, defined in the British system as Scotland's historic technological university, has taken on an even more semicomprehensive form where three of its five faculties (business, education, and the arts) are concentrated in research, teaching, and service outside science and technology. Five universities, five distinct places, conditioned by national and local contexts, different origins and developmental trajectories, and the commitment and effort of particular individuals.

But we have also seen that the institutional stories can be framed in a common conceptual structure. Formed largely from research observations, five identified elements become generalized pathways of a type of university transformation which builds upon inquiry and moves an institution aggressively into increasingly competitive orbits of science and learning. The abstracted pathways serve analytically as middle-range categories. They rise up from the realities of particular institutions to highlight features shared across a set of universities, but at the same time they still allow for local variation. Operating at only a first level of generality, the elements avoid the mists of vagueness encountered in the rarified atmosphere of unanalyzed academic abstractions and commencement-day rhetorics that clog academic and public images of how universities operate and change. My conceptual framework also shuns sweeping expressions of leadership and mission, reengineering and empowerment, strategy and stakeholding, the bromides and platitudes of the dominant management literature of the 1980s and 1990s. (Micklethwait and Wooldridge, 1996) I have stayed close to the special features of *academic* organization and have sought concreteness in the organized tools of this particular sector of society. Four elements are highly structural: we observe them in tangible offices, budgets, outreach centers, and departments. Only the more ephemeral element of institutional idea, floating in the intangible realm of intention, belief, and culture, is hard to pin down. Emphasizing manifest structures helps greatly in explaining the development of organized social systems. Without doubt, organizational change is sustained when it acquires specific carrying vehicles. Significant change in universities has definite organizational footing.

With the five-element framework in hand, pinpointing developmental pathways, we can confront a prior question: is there a generalizable *need* to transform lurking in these five cases that may also be deepening in other universities? Ambition to do more than currently could be done certainly played a major role in the examined institutions. Thoughtful administrators and faculty saw that their institution could not become all that it could be if it remained in its 1970s form; a revised posture less hobbled by imbedded constraints was required. In sensing that significant transformation was compelling, the five universities chosen for study were surely not alone. A few other institutions in Europe have similarly embarked on a transforming journey; still others around the world have had cause to contemplate major change. Confidence in the traditional ways of organizing and operating academia has been eroding.

In this concluding chapter I want to explore the reasons why other universities will find themselves treading the entrepreneurial path, *or* will ignore the need to undergo significant transformation at considerable peril. I argue that widespread features of a rapidly changing university world pressure individual institutions in many nations to become more enterprising. If multitudes of universities need to engage in the hard work of entrepreneurially led change, then the interrelated elements brought forward in our five-case analysis may be seen as answers to a global problem of growing university insufficiency.

Modern universities develop a disturbing imbalance with their environments. They face an overload of demands; they are equipped with an undersupply of response capabilities. In a demand-response equation of environment-university relationships they may be seen as falling so badly out of balance that if they remain in traditional form they move into a nearly permanent stage of disequilibrium. A tolerable balance requires a better alignment. Transforming pathways are then a means of controlling demand and enhancing response capability. To orchestrate the elements, institutional focus takes center stage.

The concept of the focused university, on which I conclude, points to a type of organizational character that growing classes of universities will need for sustainable development. In evermore turbulent settings, universities can become robust as they develop problem-solving capabilities built around a flexible focus. But to do so they must become uncommonly mindful of their characterological development. Facing complexity and uncertainty, they will have to assert themselves in new ways at the environment-university interface. But they will still have to be universities, dominated as ever by educational values rooted in the activities of research, teaching, and study.

The Demand-Response Imbalance

I remarked in the introduction to this study that national systems of higher education can neither count on returning to any earlier steady state nor of achieving a new stage of equilibrium. As principal actors within those systems, public and private universities have entered an age of turmoil for which there is no end in sight. Disjuncture is rooted in a simple fact: *demands on universities outrun their capacity to respond.* From all sides inescapable broad streams of demands rain upon the higher education system and derivatively upon specific universities within it:

- More students, and more different types of students, seek and obtain access. Ever more accessible higher education means endless "clienteles" entitled to various types of education in their lifetimes. The general trend of elite to mass to universal higher education is well-known. But its effects in creating endless demands have not been well understood. This channel of demand in itself, if left unanswered – as in the case of open-door universities on the European continent – badly overloads the response capabilities of individual institutions. And as an "environmental" demand, the clamor for inclusion is organizationally penetrating: it flows into, through, and out of universities as applicants become participants for two, four, six or eight years, and more, only to again negotiate passage as adult students in continuing education.

- More segments of the labor force demand university graduates trained for highly specialized occupations. At different degree levels, graduating students expect qualification in diverse specialties. Graduates also need retraining throughout their professional careers. Thus the training requirements for the labor force also become virtually endless. This channel of demand in itself can badly overload universities when answers have not been found to control demand and bolster response capabilities. Again, a seemingly "environmental" demand does not merely knock at the door. Rather, future careers are expressed in a vast array of training tracks and specialized student careers within the academy. "Output" boundaries are increasingly permeable.

- Patrons old and new expect more of higher education. Those in government expect more to be done at lower unit cost. It has become a virtual iron law internationally that national and regional governments will not support mass higher education at the same unit-cost level as they did for prior elite arrangements. As other patrons, particularly industry, invest in universities, their diverse expectations become pressing. Patronage shades off into a growing chorus of interest groups repeatedly expressing their voices. "Accountability" extends in many directions. This stream of demand also becomes virtually endless. And the viewpoints of the many patrons also readily cross old university boundaries as group representatives take "their" allotted places on university boards, committees, and advisory groups.

- Most important of all, *knowledge outruns resources*. No university, and no national system of universities, can control knowledge growth. With expanding knowledge in mind, science experts have long spoken of "endless frontiers." Flowing from the research imperative built into modern disciplines and interdisciplinary fields of study, knowledge expansion, *and* specialization, *and* reconfiguration are self-propelling phenomena.

The unbelievable scale and scope of just the contemporary knowledge base can be readily illustrated. As of the early-to-mid 1990s, the field of chemistry produced worldwide a million research articles in less than two years. Mathematics generated more than a hundred thousand new theorems a year. The biological sciences fragmented and recombined as well as produced new knowledge at a rate that required curricular revision of teaching materials every two to three years. Economists have turned their logics to every sector of society, rapidly creating subfields that concentrate on such topics as the economics of the family, crime, and social welfare. Psychology has become 20 and more specialties, some so large that they break away in national and international associations of their own. Historians recently produced more literature in two decades than they did in all previous periods: by proliferating such specialties as the history of science in nineteenth-century Japan, they endlessly divide attention by societal activity, historical time, and country. Throughout the humanities new points of view that contest traditional understandings have emerged in a confusing jumble, causing some humanists to see the university as an institution that has lost its soul. And the knowledge produced and circulated in universities is now greatly extended by the growing array of knowledge producers located in other sectors of society. Business schools in universities are only partly responsible for the vast outpouring of books about business management which had risen in the mid-1990s to over 2,000 a year, more than five a day.

The point is inescapable: internationally, no one controls the production, reformulation, and distribution of knowledge. Fields of knowledge are the ultimate uncontrollable force that can readily leave universities running a losing race. Just by itself, the faculty of a university, department by department, expresses an inexhaustible appetite for expansion in funding, personnel, students, and space. Rampaging knowledge is a particularly penetrating demand, rooted in the building blocks of the system: it shapes basic-unit orientation, organization, and practice. Since it has no stopping place, it never ceases. As one field of knowledge after another stretches across national boundaries and brings more parts of universities into a truly international world of science and education, growth in knowledge specialties also becomes the ultimate internationalizing force for the higher education sector of society.

These four broad streams of endless demand converge to create enormous *demand overload*. Universities are caught in a cross-fire of expectations. And all the channels of demand exhibit a high rate of change.

In the face of the increasing overload, universities find themselves limited in response capability. Traditional funding sources limit their provision of university finance: governments indicate they can pay only a decreasing share of present and future costs. "Underfunding" becomes a constant. Traditional university infrastructure becomes even more of a constraint on the possibilities of response. If left in customary form, central direction ranges between soft and soggy. Elaborated collegial authority leads to sluggish decision-making: 50 to 100 and more central committees have the power to study, delay, and veto. The senate becomes more of a bottleneck than the administration. Evermore complex and specialized, elaborated basic units – faculties, schools, and departments – tend to become separate entities with individual privileges, shaping the university into a federation in which major and minor parts barely relate to one another. Even when new departments can be added to underpin substantive growth and program changes, the extreme difficulty of terminating established academic tribes or recombining their territories insures that rigidity will dominate. Resources go to maintenance rather than to the inducement and support of change.

As demands race on, and response capability lags, institutional insufficiency results. A deprivation of capability develops to the point where timely and continuous reform becomes exceedingly difficult. Systemic crisis sets in.

How are universities near the end of the twentieth century sometimes made sufficient unto their changing environments? How are demand and response brought into reasonable balance? Adaptive responses that ease the strain take place at both system and institutional levels. System solutions set the broad context for university pathways of adaptive action.

The Search for System Solutions

National and provincial systems of higher education primarily cope with the growing demand-response imbalance by differentiation. Through both planned schemes and unplanned adjustments, systems sort out gross bundles of tasks to different types of universities, colleges, and research establishments. (Clark, 1983; Teichler, 1988; Neave, 1996; Meek et al, 1996) Formal sectors are built: in Europe, universities and polytechnics have often been set apart; in the United States, universities, four-and-five-year colleges, and two-year community colleges are commonly separated into a tripartite division of labor. Additionally, where private institutions exist, they develop individual niches in the overall national system. Access is thereby differentiated, labor market relations segmented, and different patrons provide different types and levels of support and expect different results. Beyond such broad sector separation further differentiation often occurs among universities: specialized and comprehensive universities are common in European systems.

But formal differentiation is often strongly opposed. Recently in European countries, a political tug-of-war has taken place between political parties and interest groups who want to maintain or construct an integrated, even homogeneous, single national system and those who stress the advantages of a formal division of labor. A combination of nominal integration and operational differentiation has become a useful compromise. While such institutions as polytechnics and teacher training colleges are blessed with the university title and brought into an all-encompassing single system, the differentiation of institutions, programs, and degree levels continues. The university label is stretched to give it multiple meanings and usages.

The American system offers an extreme case of the creation of different types of universities. Private institutions quite freely anoint themselves as universities; public colleges, state by state, lobby themselves into the university title. The growing aggregation of 400 or more places called universities has stretched into a half-dozen major categories: some grant many doctorates and do much research; some grant a few doctorates and do a little research; and some neither grant doctorates nor do hardly any research. (Carnegie Foundation for the Advancement of Teaching, 1994) Crossover types readily appear; e.g., some universities and colleges that are not permitted by state authorities to award doctorates proceed on their own to develop a research culture, secure more research funds than some institutions that do doctoral work, and link up with other institutions to give a joint doctorate. In Britain, after the government collapsed the old binary line and allowed polytechnics to become known as universities, the stretch in meaning of the term became much greater. A differentiation in resources and teaching and research commitments that previously took place between two main types of institutions became greater differentiation within a single formal type.

A "democratization" of titles does not bring full operational convergence: institutions become known more by what they do rather than by what they are called. Hence in national systems and on the worldwide stage we find some universities heavily concentrated on research and some that hardly do any at all; those that give many advanced degrees and others that concentrate almost completely on the first major degree; those oriented to knowledge for its own sake and those centered on useful knowledge; some that take up national roles and others situated as regional places; and on and on.

Internationally, in the 1980s and 1990s, differential effective access to sources of income rapidly became the favorite way to differentiate university systems. We have seen this national tool operate in Britain, Holland, Sweden, and Finland. Governmental mainline support with its standardizing effects is deliberately reduced or allowed to fall as a share of university costs. The system overall must turn to what we have categorized as second and third streams of support; each has largely differentiating effects. In research-grant competition, standardization gives way to winners and losers; research niches occupied by different universities offer comparative advantage. In exploiting numerous third-stream sources, universities have different possibilities set by location and historic capacity. Then as they individually maneuver, struggling to gain more resources, they widen the differences in specific configurations of external linkages. System evolution toward diversified income promotes a dynamic of institutional diversity and competition. Universities are potentially more individualized. Patrons are then all the more inclined to think they should treat unequal things unequally.

In overcoming response inadequacies, national systems of higher education can go beyond the broadbrush of the differentiation response; they can explore the utility of reforms by engaging in deliberate institutional experimentation. In Finnish higher education the process is known as "learning by experimenting." (Välimaa, 1994) There, recent experiments included the block-grant budgetary arrangement at Joensuu, the flexible workload scheme piloted at Jyväskylä, and several changes explored in other institutions in quality assessment and in the development of a new polytechnic sector. The Finns have learned that pilot experimentation is relatively easy to initiate: everyone can readily agree to have an experiment get underway "because it is meant to be only a trial and it might fail." The critical moment of "learning by experimenting," for the system at large, comes "when the supporters of the experiment want to expand it system-wide." (p. 153) Then others can coalesce in opposition around their doubts and in support of interests that might be weakened: academic labor unions have resisted in Finland when they anticipated a reduction in bargaining power and less equity in staff rewards.

One large advantage of experimentation in the search for solutions is that small-scale efforts at the outset avoid the large mistakes made when central officials mandate reforms across the entire system without preliminary testing. Since there is no way by means of prior reasoning that central planners can know enough about all local contexts and constraints, the Large Plan (or Big Bang) approach maximizes the scale and scope of unanticipated and undesired consequences. Centralized governments are biased in favor of this road to failure.

Systems of higher education are blunt instruments for reform. (For case studies that reveal bluntness in system efforts to "restructure" higher education in five American states, see MacTaggart and Associates, 1996) Using the differentiation response, systems can indeed establish broad divisions of labor, implicitly if not explicitly, that serve somewhat to limit demands made upon particular universities and colleges. Ministries and coordinating bodies can point institutions toward different combinations of programs and degrees; they can encourage different segments to adopt different doctrines supporting particular tasks. But systems acting from above have great difficulty in activating local initiatives. In western Europe the reverse has happened: system organization traditionally has worked to induce institutional passivity and weak local leadership. The national or state ministry provided administrative services and lumped together the staff of the university sector in systemwide categories of rank and salary; in effect, it created membership in a national civil service. Within the universities senior professors had commanding authority in their separate departments and institutes. This "continental mode" of state bureaucracy and faculty guild left a weak middle – the elected short-term rector assisted by only a small central staff and surrounded by congregations of powerful professors. (Clark, 1983, pp. 125–129) The "British mode" of authority structure was just a half-step away, with only modest authority located in vice-chancellorships (compared to that of American university presidents) and a web of faculty committees in and around an academic senate very involved in the consideration of change. Weak institutional steering became the norm. With some strengthening of rectorial authority and the enlarging and professionalizing of central staff, this pattern changed somewhat in many European universities in the 1970s, 1980s, and early 1990s, but not enough to constitute a sturdy response capability with which to face mounting and fast-moving demands. The weak center has severely limited the university capacity to change. Thus, the bluntness of system initiatives amidst the growing scale and complexity of the university sector has coexisted with a *structured* lack of initiative at the institutional level.

Weak capacity to balance demand and response, we should note, varies somewhat between one-faculty and multifaculty universities. Although they do not escape the problem of deepening imbalance, specialized universities are better positioned than the comprehensive institutions to control demand around their subject specialization and, with a more integrated character, to pursue an entrepreneurial response. Their subject concentration helps measurably to solve the growing problem of institutional focus. It is no mystery why in Europe or America, or elsewhere, specialized universities can more readily move toward entrepreneurial postures than comprehensive ones, particularly if their specialty is technology or business. When I sought nominations of universities for this study, it was no accident that the institutions named by knowledgeable European colleagues, including ones not chosen for study, turned out often to be specialized places, for example, the technologically oriented University of Compiègne in France, the business-administration oriented University of St. Gallen in Switzerland.

In contrast, the imbalance thesis applies strongly to comprehensive public universities. Organized around a wide array of subjects that stretches from classics to medicine, these institutions virtually promise higher officials, legislators, and the general public they will be all things for all demands. Martin Trow (1970, pp. 184–185) noted a quarter-century ago in an analysis of "elite" and "popular" functions of modern higher education that responding to external needs and demands was even then fast becoming an endless task:

> If one popular function is the provision of mass higher education to nearly everybody who applies for it, the second is the provision of useful knowledge and service to nearly every group and institution that wants it. . . the demand on the universities for such service is increasing all the time. This in part reflects the growth of the knowledge-base created by the scientific explosion of the past few decades. Not only is much of this new knowledge of potential applied value to industry, agriculture, the military, the health professions, etc., but also new areas of national life are coming to be seen as users of knowledge created in the university.

The implicit commitment of universities to embrace all of the expanding knowledge core of modern society deepened the commitment both to extend access and to service the interests of outside groups with diverse bundles of relevant knowledge and useful training. System management has been unable to control this explosion in commitments: overloaded universities have simply become more overloaded.

Other observers have also taken early note of the increasing imbalance. Based on a study of 17 universities and colleges then under stress, David Riesman warned in the 1970s against the danger of institutions overextending their resources in order to be all things to all people. (Riesman, 1973, p. 445) Two decades later, in the 1990s, the tendency to overextend resources has become more marked and the results more painful. Based on site visits and interviews in the mid-1990s at 13 colleges and universities in the American system, Leslie and Fretwell found there "was broad recognition that missions had become too loose, that too many different programs were being offered, and that scarce resources were being spread too thin across too many activities." (Leslie and Fretwell, 1996, p. xiv) Administrators and faculty "reported (and lamented) that they had made too few hard decisions" during the previous two decades. Their lament "was frequently punctuated with one phrase: 'we have tried too hard to be all things to all people,' with the unspoken trailer [that] 'we have become too diffuse to use our scarce resources well'." (p. 22) These American observers concluded that "a theme. . . ran throughout our site visits: being distinctive and purposeful is better than being all things to all people." (p. 16) And institutional strain this time, in the 1990s, was seen by participants as systemically different from periods of stress in the past: "It is a common refrain among those with whom we have consulted to suggest that things are not going to be the same this time, or ever again." (p. xii)

The differentiation response, it seems, finally comes down to the individual university. Each university has always had unique features that stem from geographic location, genetic imprints, student backgrounds, idiosyncratic historical developments, faculty strengths and weaknesses, and the play of particular personalities. Now, particularly as knowledge outruns resources, a university's basic departments are under ever greater pressure to commit to specialties that differentiate them from their peer-discipline departments at other universities, whether in physics or psychology or history. And what happens among departments and faculties radiates upward to intensify the need for entire universities to differentiate themselves in niches of knowledge, clientele, and labor market linkage. Such differentiation can be left to drift, and hence to occur slowly; but with accelerating change, the costs of drift and delay rise – the demand-response imbalance only deepens. Institutional action then has to be set in motion.

System organizers can help to clear the way by reducing state mandates and manipulating broad incentives, but only universities themselves can take the essential actions. The point was made in striking fashion by Clark Kerr in 1993 (p. 33, emphasis added) when he stressed that

> For the first time, a really international world of learning, highly competitive, is emerging. If you want to get into that orbit, you have to do so on merit. You cannot rely on politics or anything else. You have to give a good deal of autonomy to institutions for them to be dynamic and to move fast in international competition. *You have to develop entrepreneurial leadership to go along with institutional autonomy.*

Enter the growing necessity of what we can now call "the entrepreneurial response."

The Entrepreneurial Response

If the state and other external patrons cannot exercise the required initiative, how can universities shift from a passive to an active mode? As historically constituted, their internal faculties and departments cannot separately do the job. Oversight of their particular fields and protection of their own material interests has been their customary mandate. Only an overall organizational realignment, constructed in a first approximation by the elements captured in this study, can set into motion a new highly active mode. The five cases and certain relevant studies can help to place those elements in the broader framework of the imbalance thesis.

The strengthened steering core

Warwick, Twente, Strathclyde, Chalmers, Joensuu – all exhibited in 1995 a greater systematic capacity to steer themselves than they had possessed 15 years earlier. That ability did not take any one form. It could be relatively centralized or decentralized, generally appearing in practice as a locally unique combination of the two – a "centralized decentralization." (Henkel, 1997, p. 137) At a given time this evolving steering capability appeared in different institutions at different stages of development and in degree. It could have been initiated by strong-minded change agents, figures drawn to leadership positions from within or without who wished to break the cake of custom. But in the sustained work of implementation such personal leadership commonly gave way to collegial groups. Stronger line authority also appeared: rector's office to dean to department head, or, in flat structures that bypass deans, from center to department head. Individuals and groups were held accountable.

Most important, the administrative backbone fused new managerial values with traditional academic ones. Management points of view, including the notion of entrepreneurship, were carried from center to academic heartland, while faculty values infiltrated the managerial space. The blending of perspectives worked best when academics who were trusted by peers served in central councils and took up responsibility for the entire institution. Since the underlying traditional academic culture cannot be ignored, cannot be pushed aside, it must be put to work and thereby adapted. Central faculty involvement became a crucial step in avoiding what the academic staff would otherwise see as hard managerialism, too much top-down command. In the hard work of transformation in these cases and elsewhere, much depends on how well managerial and faculty values become intertwined and then expressed in daily operating procedures.

Whatever its shape, the strengthened managerial core consists of agents who work to find resources for the institution as a whole. They seek other patrons instead of waiting passively for the government to return to full funding. They work to diversify income and thereby enlarge the pool of discretionary money. They seek out new infrastructure units that reach across old university boundaries to link up more readily than traditional departments with outside establishments, especially industrial firms. The core gives the institution a greater collective ability to make hard choices among fields of knowledge, backing some to the disadvantage of others; this in turn shapes access possibilities and job-market connections. The strengthened steering mechanism is necessary for the task of cross-subsidizing among the university's many fields and degree levels, taxing rich programs to aid less-fortunate ones that otherwise would be relegated to the corner or even dropped from the enterprise because they cannot pay their way. Agents of the core thereby not only seek to subsidize new activities but also try to enhance old valuable programs in the academic heartland. As much maneuvering among contradictory demands becomes necessary, the agents of the constructed core become institutionally responsible for doing so.

A strengthened administrative core, then, is a mandatory feature of a heightened capability to confront the root imbalance of modern universities.

The enhanced development periphery

The new peripheries that enterprising universities construct also take quite different specific forms. They variously consist of outreach administrative units that promote contract research, contract education, and consultancy. They include a varied array of research centers that are generally, but not always, multi- or transdisciplinary. The new units and centers may be closely or loosely linked to the steering core and the heartland departments. Like science parks that become autonomous, some peripheral units may have the name and sponsorship of the university but then operate much like mediating institutions situated between the university and outside organizations. Again, there is no one way, no one model to emulate.

But the developmental peripheries we have observed have a valuable common outcome: they move a university toward a dual structure of basic units in which traditional departments are supplemented by centers linked to the outside world. The matrix-like structure becomes a tool for handling the inevitable growth of the service role of universities. Department-based "specialist groups" are complemented by "project groups" that admit external definitions of research problems and needed training. The new groups cross old lines of authority; they promote environmental linkages in their daily practice. We noted at Chalmers that they can even effect reciprocal knowledge transfer; the university learns from outside firms as the companies learn from the university. The matrix structure allows for more temporary units, thereby introducing flexibility amidst stability. With tenured staff mainly based in the departments and nontenured and part-time staff often predominating in the outreach centers, the more temporary units of the periphery are more readily disbanded.

Since units of a developmental periphery extend, cross, and blur boundaries, they can decisively shape the long-run character of a university. They can develop new competencies close to useful problem solving. They can generate income that helps to diversify funding. They answer the call for interdisciplinary efforts. But if not judged by academic values as well as managerial and budgetary interests for their appropriateness in a university, they can move an institution toward the character of a shopping mall. A connected and somewhat focused construction of the periphery requires a collective institutional capacity to make choices based on educational values. New outward-looking units can make the problem of overall institutional focus all the more difficult: research centers contend with old departments, transdisciplinary perspectives with disciplinary orientations, the useful with the basic, the outward-looking with the inward-oriented. But when carefully monitored, the periphery becomes a second virtually essential element with which to lessen the imbalance between environmental demands and response capacity. Traditional departments alone cannot effect all the needed linkages: in themselves, they cannot add up to an effective focus. The new periphery is necessary, even if it adds to the organized complexity of the university.

As a halfway house to the outside world, the developmental periphery becomes an organized location within a university for the entry and absorption of whole new modes of thinking. In ideal typical terms formulated by an international study group in the mid-1990s, their designated "Mode 1" refers to the traditional way of handling knowledge in disciplinary frameworks. A newly emerging "Mode 2," transdisciplinary and problem-oriented, was seen by the study group as located largely outside universities in a host of knowledge-centered enterprises that stretch from major industrial laboratories to policy think tanks to management consultancies to new small and medium-sized enterprises. (Gibbons et al, 1994; see also Ziman, 1994) Between the ideal types there lies a lengthy continuum of different practical combinations. The peripheries of universities we observed in this study incorporate much Mode 2. Their units are established precisely to go beyond disciplinary definitions; they extend university boundaries to bring in the perspectives of outside problem-solving groups; they are prepared to take their leads from the outside and to work close to application. They are often strongly committed to the straight-on production of useful knowledge.

An enhanced developmental periphery plays many roles in enterprising universities, not the least in bringing new modes of thinking and problem solving within newly stretched boundaries. Organizationally, in Peter Scott's terms, it helps to stretch the "core" university into the "distributed" university, where knowledge, the primary commodity, is more "applications-generated." (Scott, 1997, pp. 11–14)

The discretionary funding base

Demand overload hits hard at the core support of universities. Student growth and knowledge growth together increase enormously the costs of systems of higher education and individual universities. Higher costs then change the relationship of universities to their principal patrons, especially funding ministries. If higher education in earlier days had been a minor charge in governmental budgets, it now becomes a major expenditure. As a big-ticket item, university support moves up the agenda of governmental concerns and is thrown into direct competition with other major interests. Politicians pay attention. They put universities on their personal and party agendas. The sheer happenstance of where university support is decided in the state bureaucratic and legislative structure can even become critical, variously contending with the major sums sought by schools, welfare agencies, health departments, prisons, agricultural interests, and the military. Even in good times of rising state income and outlay, governments then seek to control higher education costs. In bad times of general retrenchment they insist on major cuts. They issue dire warnings in statements that echo internationally that the future will bring even more constraint. Government becomes an uneven patron, often acting like a sometime purchaser of university services; it can hardly be depended on in the long term. Its own changing agenda will at times give overwhelming priority to coping with depression, national debt, and international entanglements.

Traditional universities come to a fork in the financial road. They can passively fall in line and undergo parallel financial increases and decreases – as the government goes, so they go – with the governmental stimulus determining university response; or they can actively intervene by deciding to develop additional lines of income from pursued patrons. University ambition encourages the second choice, competition virtually demands it. Such budgetary activity is a crucial step in university entrepreneurship. Active cost containment is also then given a high priority by the institution itself, from central staff to the many departments and units in the academic heartland and the developmental periphery.

To build a diversified funding base in a university is to construct a portfolio of patrons to share rising costs. As new patrons contribute, their expectations of what they should get in return readily intrude to become new constraints. Universities then need greater self-consciousness on where they draw the line between what they are willing to do and not do to meet those demands. The collective will, located in the steering core, then comes into play to define new limits around greatly expanded boundaries; heartland departments also have to test their own edges of legitimacy.

But whatever the relations with specific patrons, a diversified funding base enhances university discretion. The enlarged portfolio of income streams increases total resources. It allows a university to "roll with the punches"; a loss here is replaced by a gain there. It allows a university to build reserves (and to borrow monies) and then to take innovative steps, as Warwick did when it used accumulated surpluses from its earned income to fund a new, striking research fellowship scheme. Diversity in financing, it now appears, "can be regarded as a prerequisite for adaptability." (Hölttä, 1995, p. 56) The multistream financial base enhances the evermore important capacity to cross-subsidize internally: top-slicing and redistribution of funds by central committees tap the monies brought in by some fields and activities to aid others judged to be necessary and needy. Cross-subsidy becomes the financial heart of university integration. (Massy, 1994; Williams, 1995)

The internal disposition of funds raised through diversified sources is always contentious and never permanently solved. Professors and departments active in bringing in money do not like to see some of it passed off to others who are not, especially if the other departments appear to be lost in mists of conceptual ambiguity, even bogged down in self-imposed disarray. The greater the internal dispersion of fields and interests, the greater the need to have the haves help the have-nots. *And* the more contentious the issue of internal redistribution becomes. Comprehensive universities have great difficulty in moving money across the gulf between, for example, physics and classics as specific fields or more broadly between engineering and the humanities. Cross-subsidization may flow from teaching to research, or in some cases in the reverse direction. It may flow across levels of education, from undergraduate to graduate, or the other way around. Certainly a primary issue in diversified funding, it is central to the making of choices leading to better focused universities.

The stimulated heartland

Since universities consist of widely divergent fields in their traditional departments, enterprising action typically spreads unevenly in the old heartland. Science and technology departments commonly become entrepreneurial first and most fully. Social science departments, aside from economics and business, find the shift more difficult and commonly lag behind. Humanities departments have good reason to be resisting laggards: new money does not readily flow their way from either governmental or nongovernmental patrons. Deliberate effort on their part to go out and raise funds by offering new services may seem particularly out of place, even demeaning. Since departmental adoption of an entrepreneurial attitude will normally vary, a university that has partially transformed itself to be more enterprising might largely exist in a schizophrenic state, entrepreneurial on one side and traditional on the other. Administrators and faculty at the five universities studied rejected this option. Schizophrenic character did not appeal to them: it suggested a split that would mean endless, bitter contention. If that were to be the outcome, then the move into entrepreneurial action might well be more trouble than it was worth: doubters in other universities would be right.

Overall scale and scope are perhaps decisive here. Small to middle size universities – 6,000 to approximately 13,000 in our five cases – are still positioned to seek a unified character, even if they stretch from microbiology to folklore. An integrated identity has much to offer: perceivable gains outweigh apparent losses. But large universities of 20,000, 30,000, 50,000 and more, particularly when organized in large stand-alone faculties or schools – the dominant form in Europe and in much of the world – might well find that entrepreneurial habits do not spread well across their major parts. They might then be forced to operate with an entrepreneurial/traditional split in character, with minimal interaction and little or no cross-subsidy across major components. The entrepreneurial side could depend on diversified income and look to new forms of outreach and knowledge production. The traditional side could depend on mainline allocation based on student enrolment and degree output as the foundation for the future.

Impressive in the universities studied was the extent to which the heartland departments had bought into entrepreneurial change. Their changeover has not been easy, not even in the specialized institutions most fully based on science and technology. Even in science departments professors may be committed to knowledge for its own sake in a way that excludes applied interests. But the distinction between basic and applied has steadily blurred and science departments can typically find foci that combine the two. In the social sciences and humanities, as we have seen, departments also find new ways to be educationally useful as they relate to new demands with, for example, policy analysis and multimedia explorations. One traditional department after another finds educational as well as economic value in becoming a more enterprising basic unit.

Stimulated academic departments must find ways to fuse their new administrative capability and outreach mentality with traditional outlooks in their fields. Academic norms operate close to the surface: they define whether changes are "up-market" or "down-market." Departmental entrepreneurship that leads to shoddy goods, as defined by other academics, can readily set in motion a vicious circle of declining reputation and less selective recruitment of staff and students. Departments have to make clear that they are not willing to respond to all demands that swirl around them in their respective fields of activities – from potential students, young and old, industrial firms and professional associations, local, regional, national, and international governmental departments. They have to select and thereby to focus. When carried out effectively, a widespread embodiment of entrepreneurship in a university strengthens *selective* substantive growth in its basic units.

The entrepreneurial belief

The most difficult part of this study's analysis was to grasp organizational ideas and beliefs and relate them to structures that support processes of change. A long-standing popular misconception places a Great Person with a Large Idea at the front end of change. A modern derivative of this view depicts a chief executive officer or management team formulating at the outset a global strategic plan. Idea becomes purpose, a mission statement soon follows, and all else becomes means to a prechosen end. But the reality of change in complex organizations, especially in universities, is different. New, institutionally defining ideas are typically tender and problematic at the outset of an important change. They must be tested, worked out, and reformulated. If they turn out to be utopian, they are soon seen as counterproductive wishful thinking. If found to be excessively opportunistic, they provide no guidance: any adjustment will do. Ideas become realistic and capable of some steering as they reflect organizational capability and tested environmental possibilities. New organizational ideas are but symbolic experiments in the art of the possible.

An institutional *idea* that makes headway in a university has to spread among many participants and link up with other ideas. As the related ideas become expressed in numerous structures and processes, and thereby endure, we may see them as institutional *beliefs* that stress distinctive ways. Successful entrepreneurial beliefs, stressing a will to change, can in time spread to embrace much and even all of an institution, becoming a new *culture*. What may have started out as a simple or naive idea becomes a self-asserting shared view of the world offering a unifying *identity*. A transformed culture that contains a sense of historical struggle can in time even become a *saga*, an embellished story of successful accomplishment. Our five universities have moved along this ideational road.

Such cultural transformation at Warwick started out in the early 1980s with the tender idea that it would "earn" its way. With growing success, the earned income approach became a sturdy belief that here was an unusual British university aggressively developing new sources of income, new patterns of organization, and new productive relationships with the outside world. True believers dominated the steering core and became more numerous in a campuswide culture. Outsiders took special note. By its twenty-fifth year, the university was uncommonly well-equipped symbolically to celebrate itself with an enriched story of "the Warwick way." An organizational saga was emerging.

Twente started its move in the early 1980s with an almost defiant assertion that it was "*the* entrepreneurial university," hardly knowing what that would mean in practice. It turned out to mean that Twente would develop a strengthened managerial core and a newly devised developmental periphery and the other operational elements this study has identified. Spreading out in the academic heartland, the initial simply stated idea became an embedded belief, then a widespread culture. By the mid-1990s this small place claimed a rugged identity formed around a recent history of largely successful struggle: a saga was on its way. Twente came to believe in itself to the point of making vigorous efforts to spread its particular attitudes and special operational forms to others: it took up leadership in an emerging small circle of European self-defined "innovative universities."

The leading idea at Strathclyde in the early 1980s was not sharply formulated. A new vice-chancellor felt strongly that the place had to become more managerial, more businesslike, more able to stand on its own feet. If it were to prosper it had to be run differently. In time, the initial managerial idea, expressed in a distinctive central steering group, a productive periphery, and an entrepreneurial "spirit" in some heartland departments became folded into a generalized belief system of "useful learning." This doctrine embraced two hundred years of development while it asserted a will to work with industry and government to solve current problems. The Strathclyde doctrine of useful learning only needed to be slightly embellished and romanticized, as exemplified in the bicentennial celebration I described, in order to become an organizational saga.

Chalmers self-consciously began to assert in the early 1980s a commitment to "innovation." As the idea and related practices were worked out, a sense of difference grew. A long-standing Chalmers "spirit" was intensified to become an embracing culture that helped predispose the institution to take up in 1994 the highly unusual status of a foundation university, an institutional definition that nearly all other Swedish universities were unable or unwilling to consider. The sense of distinctiveness was thereby further extended, intensifying overall identity. In this ideational part of the quest, deeply rooted cultural features have become parts of a Chalmers saga in which past developments, current intentions, and future character are depicted as closely linked. Chalmers enthusiasts could readily say in the mid-1990s that their place was something different in the state of Sweden. They also had confident reason to believe that a similar entrepreneurial culture will increasingly appear in other Swedish universities.

Joensuu in the mid-1980s took to an idea of becoming a pilot institution that would experiment with an important basic change for the entire Finnish national system of universities. In its national setting the idea of doubly decentralizing budget-based control all the way down to the department level was a radical one. Joensuu effected the idea to the point of departmental dominance. Early acceptance of a second idea, piloted at another university, that of flexible workloads, helped to make the institution significantly different from those operating in traditional Finnish style. As the "piloting" ideas worked their way into the fabric of the institution, Joensuu has grown up symbolically as well as physically, strengthening its sense of self and its place in the world.

*   *   *   *

We have noted repeatedly throughout this study that the five elements of transformation become just that by means of their interaction. Each by itself can hardly make a significant difference. Those who see universities from the top-down might readily assume that the strengthened steering core is the leading element. But a newly constituted management group, for example, is soon without teeth if discretionary funds are not available, new units in the periphery cannot be constructed, heartland departments fall into opposition, and the group's idea of a transformed institution gains no footing. The interaction of transforming elements also largely takes place incrementally over a number of years. Our results accord strongly with an incrementalist view of organizational change. (Lindblom, 1959, 1979; Redner, ed., 1993) Particularly for universities, we stress *interactive instrumentalism*. Transformation requires a structured change capability and development of an overall internal climate receptive to change. As we have seen by reviewing development over ten to 15 year periods, the building of structural capability and cultural climate takes time and is incrementally fashioned. Action taken at the center requires faculty involvement and approval. Change in new and old units in the periphery and in the heartland is piecemeal, experimental, and adaptive. The operational units, departments and research centers, remain the sites where research, teaching, and service are performed: what they do and do not do becomes finally central. As put sharply by David W. Leslie (1996, p. 110) in arguing against linear-rational views of strategic planning: "change in colleges and universities comes when it happens in the trenches; what faculty and students do is what the institution becomes. It does not happen because a committee or a president asserts a new idea."

Even in the business world, we may note, careful analysts who trace organizational change over many years observe that successful firms essentially engage in "cumulative incrementalism": they inch forward by making rapid partial changes. Firms choose to "spread and minimize risks by initiating many different projects," rather than try to engage in large-scale strategic change. (Stopford and Baden-Fuller, 1994, p. 523) They engage in "concentric entrepreneurialism." Even in business, leadership is depicted as a diffused phenomenon: "Leadership is acutely context sensitive. . . The need may be for more than one leader over time if performance is to be maintained. Equally important may be the creation of collective leadership at a senior level. . . which may then be supported by the development of a sense of complementary leadership at lower levels. Leading change involves action by people at every level of the business." (Pettigrew & Whipp, 1991, pp. 280–281) And from a third careful business analyst: "Capabilities grow through the actions of the members of the firm – through the behaviors of employees at all organizational levels." (Leonard-Barton, 1995, p. 28)

Such findings from sustained analysis of business firms over years of development concur with developmental studies of universities: leadership can be an attribute of groups; entrepreneurship is a phenomenon of total organizations and their many collective parts. "The entrepreneurial response" on which we have concentrated is an all-university capability.

The Focused University

The entrepreneurial response to the growing imbalance in the environment-university relationship gives universities a better chance to control their own destinies. The response may be seen as a way to recover the autonomy lost, particularly in public universities, when mounting demands began to dominate the capacity of universities to respond. The new autonomy is different from the old. In an earlier day autonomous public universities could be given full state support and largely left alone to educate a few students, engage in limited basic research, and prepare professionals for several fields of work. When only one young person in 20 sought university training, most people most of the time did not think about what the university was doing and what it could do for them. Fields of research were simpler, knowledge growth, while moving at a striking pace, could still be grasped. As the end of the twentieth century approaches, however, the demand side of the environment-university relationship has spun out of control and institutional response has become increasingly insufficient. Now when virtually everyone can demand some involvement or relationship, loosely coupled universities have offered ad hoc, diffuse responses.

Universities are caught up in grand contradictions: with less money, do more and more; maintain as always the expanding cultural heritage, the best of the past, but quickly and flexibly develop new fields of study and modes of thought; relate to everyone's demand because all are "stakeholders." An American university president crisply formulated in the mid-1990s that the modern research university (public *and* private) has become "overextended, underfocused; overstressed, underfunded." (Vest, 1995) Alert rectors and vice-chancellors in Europe could readily agree, recognizing that not only can the condition of underfunded lead to a sense of being overstressed, but that "underfocused" and "overextended" may be virtually two sides of the same institutional posture.

The entrepreneurial response offers a formula for institutional development that puts autonomy on a self-defined basis: diversify income to increase financial resources, provide discretionary money, *and* reduce governmental dependency; develop new units outside traditional departments to introduce new environmental relationships and new modes of thought and training; convince heartland departments that they too can look out for themselves, raise money, actively choose among specialties, and otherwise take on an entrepreneurial outlook; evolve a set of overarching beliefs that guide and rationalize the structural changes that provide a stronger response capability; and build a central steering capacity to make large choices that help focus the institution. The entrepreneurial response in all its fullness gives universities better means for redefining their reach – to include more useful knowledge, to move more flexibly over time from one program emphasis to another, and finally to build an organizational identity and focus. Warwick, Twente, Strathclyde, Chalmers, and Joensuu have all in somewhat different specific ways shown us how to focus university reach.

Universities need foci that help them solve the problem of severe imbalance and to define anew their societal usefulness. They need to find sustainable niches in the ecology of a knowledge industry that becomes more international and more dispersed among institutions outside formal higher education. The difficulties are huge. Comprehensive universities, those of wide scope, in Europe, America, and elsewhere will remain under great popular and governmental pressure to cover the broadest possible range of subjects and interests. Scattering their promises, and in many cases unable to cap their size, they will continue to tend to spread in a virtually uncontrolled fashion. They take on even more tasks and expectations, undercutting the possibilities of building a critical mass of resources, faculty, and students in different basic units. To contain unbridled comprehensiveness, choices have to be made about the relative magnitude of beginning and advanced levels of study, different services to clienteles and occupations, and especially about fields of knowledge to highlight and downplay. And within every field choices have to be made to pursue certain specialties while ignoring others. If such choices are not made, then all units and subunits simply receive fair shares on the downslope of limited resources and hardened structures. Steering is left to the mercy of sunk costs.

As active university postures come to the fore, we find they can have positive effects on university character that are not anticipated in traditional thought. The entrepreneurial pathways tend to build coherence. A university becomes more willing to assert to the outside world that it is different, even distinctive. The whole institution can legitimately claim that it has its act together and is thereby better prepared to cope with the confusing complexity and rising uncertainty characteristic of modern higher education. A reputation of coherent competence provides a symbolic bridge to the environment for a favorable gathering of money, staff, and students.

As entrepreneurial responses multiply, universities become more individualized. To make the point in striking fashion, that higher education is not one thing and it has no one future, the Carnegie Council of the 1970s entitled their last report on the U.S. system *Three Thousand Futures.* (Carnegie Council, 1980) Actively forming their own character in different specific contexts, and developing different specific strengths and weaknesses, entrepreneurial universities, anywhere in the world, similarly develop their own distinctive futures. Rather than praising homogeneity, they put their trust in diversified capability – a posture appropriate for an evermore complex and competitive domain.

An entrepreneurial achievement of distinctiveness serves internally to unify an identity and thereby, ironically, to rebuild a sense of community. "Entrepreneur" may continue to be a negative term in the minds of traditional academics, all the more so after they have seen hard managerialism in action. They may go on thinking of entrepreneurship as raw individualistic striving that is socially divisive. They may continue to fear that a traditional academic community, assumed to exist, will be fragmented if entrepreneurial behavior takes over. However, diffuse in structure and fragmented in intent, traditional European universities, and many others around the world, have had little or no common symbolic and material integration. What integration they have had is steadily eroded by increasing scale and scope. Collective entrepreneurship overcomes their scattered character, leading toward a more integrated self. When entire departments and faculties are assertive, and especially when a whole university takes on an entrepreneurial character, the old understandings are turned upside down. Academic groups, small and large, then see themselves in common situations with common problems, common allies, and common enemies, and in need of common action. A common culture grows, an identity is shared.

Collegiality is then put to work in a different way. Bernard J. Shapiro (President, McGill University) and Harold T. Shapiro (President, Princeton University) have cogently argued that collegiality is normally "biased in favor of the status quo – not to mention the status quo ante." The challenge is "to redefine our understandings and commitment so that, in empirical terms, collegiality and difficult choices are not mutually exclusive." (1995, p. 10) The collective forms of entrepreneurship captured in this study change the equation. They put collegiality to work in the service of hard choices. Collegiality then looks to the future. It becomes biased in favor of change.

Self-defining, self-regulating universities have much to offer. Not least is their capacity in difficult circumstances to recreate an academic community. Toward such universities, the entrepreneurial response leads the way.

References

Chapter 1: Entrepreneurial Pathways of University Transformation

Babbidge, H.D. and Rosenzweig, R. 1962 *The Federal Interest in Higher Education.* New York: McGraw-Hill.

Clark, B.R. (1995a) *Places of Inquiry: Research and Advanced Education in Modern Universities.* Berkeley and Los Angeles: University of California Press.

(1995b) Leadership and innovation in universities: from theory to practice. *Tertiary Education and Management* 1(1): 7–11.

(1996) Case studies of innovative universities: a progress report. *Tertiary Education and Management* 2(1): 52–61.

Chapter 2: The Warwick Way

Becher, T. (1993) Graduate education in Britain: the view from the ground. In: B.R. Clark (ed.) *The Research Foundations of Graduate Education: Germany, Britain, France, United States, Japan.* Berkeley and Los Angeles: University of California Press, pp. 115–153.

Bertelsmann Foundation (1990) Letter to the University of Warwick. University files.

Briggs Lord Asa (1991) A founding father reflects. *Higher Educ. Q.* 45: 311–332.

Burgess, B. (1996) Born in the USA. *Managing HE* 2: 10–12.

Burgess, R. and Schratz, M. (eds.) (1994) *International Perspectives in Postgraduate Education and Training.* Innsbruck, Austria: Österreichischer StudienVerlag.

Clark, B.R. (1995) *Places of Inquiry: Research and Advanced Education in Modern Universities.* Berkeley and Los Angeles: University of California Press.

Economist, The (12 Nov. 1994) Dosh for dons.

Economist, The (1 Nov. 1995) The professor of product development.

Griffiths, A.P. (1991) The new universities: the humanities. *Higher Educ. Q.* 45: 333–345.

Hirsh, W. (1982) Postgraduate training of researchers. In: G. Oldham (ed.) (1982) *The Future of Research.* Guildford: The Society for Research into Higher Education, pp. 190–209.

Jones, D.R. (1988) *The Origins of Civic Universities: Manchester, Leeds & Liverpool.* London: Routledge.

London Times (13 Sept. 1994) University of Warwick Science Park: 22–23.

Perkin, H. (1991) Dream, myth and reality: new universities in England, 1960–1990. *Higher Educ. Q.* 45: 294–310.

Pettigrew, A. and Ferlie, E. (1996) Some research challenges facing Warwick. Warwick University paper for discussion. University files.

Shattock, M. (1989) Memorandum to the Bertelsmann Foundation. University files.

(1994a) Optimising university resources. Paper delivered to the Conference of European Rectors, Apr. 1994.

(1994b) *The UGC and the Management of British Universities.* Buckingham, England: SRHE and Open University Press.

Thompson, E.P. (ed.) (1970) *Warwick University Ltd: Industry, Management and the Universities.* Harmondsworth, England: Penguin Books.

Thompson, Sir Michael (1991) The natural sciences in the new universities. *Higher Educ. Q.* 45:346–353.

Times Higher Education Supplement (*THES*, also known as "The Higher")

(15 Apr. 1994) Grooming graduate schools.

(5 Aug. 1994) New schools of thought.

(30 Sept. 1994) Short change.

(27 Jan. 1995) Warwick joins fellowship elite.

(5 Mar. 1995) University of Surrey: Investing in excellence.

(5 May 1995) Warwick leads as others follow.

(23 June 1995) Oxbridge dominates Warwick fellowships.

University of Warwick (1991) *Making a University: A Celebration of Warwick's First 25 Years.* Coventry.

(1992–93) *Graduate School Annual Report.*

(22 Nov. 1993a) Letter to Industrial Development Office from inno GMbH, Karlsruhe, Germany. University files.

(1993b) *Research at Warwick Business School: Interests and Publications.* Coventry.

(1994a) Warwick Business School Brochure. Coventry, 5 p.

(1944b) Warwick Manufacturing Group 1994 Summary brochure. Coventry, 2 p.

(1995a) *Annual Report. Volume 1.* Coventry.

(1995b) *Business School Annual Report 1995.* Volume 2. Coventry.

(1995c) *Graduate School Prospectus 1995. Coventry.*

(1995d) Warwick Manufacturing Group, *Excellence with Relevance.* Coventry.

(1995e) *University of Warwick Science Park: Annual Report.* Coventry.

(1996) *Warwick Research Fellowships 1994–95.* Report prepared by Dawn Duddridge. Coventry.

Chapter 3: The Twente Response

Daalder, H. (1982) The Netherlands: universities between the 'new democracy' and the 'new management.' In: H Daalder and E Shils (eds.) *Universities, Politicians and Bureaucrats: Europe and the United States.* Cambridge: Cambridge University Press, pp. 173–231.

Frijhoff, W. (1992) The Netherlands. In: B.R. Clark and G. Neave (eds.) *The Encyclopedia of Higher Education. Volume 1, National Systems of Higher Education.* Oxford: Pergamon, pp. 491–504.

Maassen, P.A.M. and van Buchem, M.T.E. (1990) Turning problems into opportunities: the University of Twente. In: F A Schmidtlein and T H Milton (eds.) *Adapting Strategic Plans to Campus Realities.* San Francisco: Jossey Bass, pp. 55–68.

Schutte, F. (1994) The University of Twente: *entrepreneurial* and *intrapreneurial* university. Paper prepared for British Council seminar, Danbury Park Conference Centre, 18 May 1994.

Science (2 Feb. 1996) The Netherlands: government pushes students onto the fast track.
Times Higher Education Supplement (THES) (24 May 1996) Opinion: a little extra ordinary.
University of Twente (1991) *Strategic Plan 1991.*
  (1995a) *Chemical Technology: Scientific Report 1991–1995.*
  (1995b) *TRD: Transfer, Research & Development*; and *TRD Information.*
  (1995c) *TSM: General Information.*
  (1996) *Liaison Group.*

Chapter 4: The Strathclyde Phenomenon

Arbuthnott, J.P. and Bone, T.R. (1993) Anatomy of a merger. *Higher Educ Q.* 47(2): 103–119.
Ashby, E. (1958, 1966) *Technology and the Academics: An Essay on Universities and the Scientific Revolution.* New York: St. Martin's Press.
Barbanel, J.C. (1993) It seemed a good idea at the time. *J of Med. Engr. & Technology* 17(5): 183–185.
Butt, J. (1996) *John Anderson's Legacy: The University of Strathclyde and its Antecedents 1796–1996.* East Linton, Scotland: Tuckwell Press in association with The University of Strathclyde.
Clark, B.R. (1995) *Places of Inquiry: Research and Advanced Education in Modern Universities.* Berkeley and Los Angeles: University of California Press.
Committee of Vice-Chancellors and Principals (CVCP) (1985) *Report of the Steering Committee for Efficiency Studies in Universities* (The Jarrett Report). London: CVCP.
Courtney, J.M. (1993) Artificial organs and biomaterials. *J of Med. Engr. & Technology* 17(5): 188–190.
Hills, G. (1981) (Strathclyde) *University Gazette.* Statement on the future by the principal.
Kelly, T. (1957) *George Birkbeck: Pioneer of Adult Education.* Liverpool: Liverpool University Press.
Paul, J.P. (1993) Bioengineering at the University of Strathclyde. *J of Med. Engr. & Technology* 17(5): 185–188.
Sanderson, M. (ed.) (1975) *The Universities in the Nineteenth Century.* London: Routledge & Kegan Paul.
Times Higher Education Supplement (THES) (1 Nov. 1996) How the universities made their money in 1994–95.
University of Strathclyde (1986) *Report of the Committee on the Organisation and Effectiveness of Decision-Making.*
  undated, early (1990s) *The Strathclyde Phenomenon.*
  (1994) Department of Electronic and Electrical Engineering. *Departmental Review* 1994.
  (1994–95) *Institutional Plan 1994–95.*
  (1996a) *Perspectives: A Place of Useful Learning.*
  (1996b) SIDR Conference presentation prepared and delivered by James Houston, Deputy Director, Research and Development Services.
  (1996c) *Faculty of Science: Presentation to Court.*
West, P.A. (1996a) Funding universities – the management challenge. *Higher Educ. Management* 8(1): 125–131.
  (1996b) A case study of the University of Strathclyde in Scotland. (Paper delivered at the International Conference on the Role of Universities in Development of Local Communities) Lodz, Poland, 14–15 June 1996.

Chapter 5: The Chalmers Thrust

Chalmers University of Technology
(1993) Office of the President. Gothenburg, Sweden.

(1994) *Chalmers Science Park*. Gothenburg, Sweden.

(1994–95) *Annual Report*. Gothenburg, Sweden.

(1994,1995) *CIC Annual Reports*. Gothenburg, Sweden.

(1995) *Freedom with Responsibility: Interview with the President*. Gothenburg, Sweden.

(1995–96) *Chalmers Advanced Management Programs (CHAMPS), Executive Programs*. Gothenburg, Sweden.

Elzinga, A. (1993) Universities, research and the transformation of the state in Sweden. In: S Rothblatt and B. Wittrock (eds.) *The European and American University Since 1800: Historical and Sociological Essays*. Cambridge: Cambridge University Press, pp. 191–233.

Geiger, R.L. (1986) *Private Sectors in Higher Education: Structure, Function and Change in Eight Countries*. Ann Arbor: University of Michigan Press.

Lane, J.E. (1992) Sweden. In: B R Clark and G Neave (eds.) *The Encyclopedia of Higher Education*, Volume I. Oxford: Pergamon Press, pp. 687–698.

Organisation for Economic Co-operation and Development (OECD) 1995 *Reviews of National Policies for Education: Sweden*. Paris: OECD.

Samuelson, U. and Samuelson, A. (1993) *Det Gamla Chalmers, 1829–1937*. Göteborg: Chalmers tekniska högskola.

Science (31 Mar. 1995) Swedish science: political spat threatens funding for basic research: 1901.

Times Higher Education Supplement (THES) (7 June 1996) Swedes switch rules: 11.

University of Gothenburg (1996) *Students' Guide*.

Chapter 6: The Joensuu Reform

Becher, T. (1989) *Academic Tribes and Territories: Intellectual Enquiry and the Cultures of Disciplines*. Milton Keynes, England: The Society for Research into Higher Education & Open University Press.

Becher, T. and Kogan, M. (1980) *Process and Structure in Higher Education*. London: Heinemann. (1992) *Process and Structure in Higher Education*. 2nd ed. London: Routledge.

Brennan, J. (1986) Peer review and partnership. *International J. of Institutional Management in Higher Education* 10(2).

Clark, B.R. (1983) *The Higher Education System: Academic Organization in Cross-National Perspective*. Berkeley and Los Angeles: University of California Press.

European Forest Institute (1995) *Annual Report*. Joensuu, Finland.

The Finnish Forest Research Institute (1996) *Joensuu Research Station Brochure*. Joensuu.

The Finnish Society of Forest Science (1995) *Research in Forest and Wood Science in Finland*. Helsinki: Helsinki University Printing House.

Halonen, M., Hölttä, S. and Pulliainen, K. (1993) Executive information services: an integrating element in decentralized university management. Paper presented at 15th Annual EAIR Forum, Turku, Finland, 15–17 Aug. 1993.

Hölttä, S. (1995) *Towards the Self-Regulative University*. (Publications in Social Sciences No. 23) Joensuu, Finland: University of Joensuu.

Hölttä, S. and Karjalainen, K. (1997) Cybernetic institutional management: theory and practice – a system of flexible workload for university teachers. *Tertiary Education and Management* 3. (Forthcoming).

Hölttä, S. and Nuotio, J. (1995) Academic leadership in a self-regulative environment: a challenge for Finnish universities. *Tertiary Education and Management* 1(1): 12–20.

Hölttä, S. and Pulliainen, K. (1992) Improving managerial effectiveness at the University of Joensuu, Finland (draft report). Paris: IIEP Research and Studies Programme, UNESCO International Institute for Educational Planning. (1993) The model of an entrepreneurial university: a challenge. Paper presented at the Annual EAIR Forum, Turku, Finland, 15–17 Aug. 1993

Kivinen, O. and Rinne, R. (1991) How to steer student flows and higher education: the headache facing the Finnish ministry of education. In: G Neave and F A Van Vught (eds.) *Prometheus Bound: The Changing Relationship Between Government and Higher Education in Western Europe.* Oxford: Pergamon Press, pp 51–63.

Ministry of Education (Finland) (1994a) *Higher Education Policy in Finland.* Helsinki.

(1994b) *University Research in Finland.* Helsinki.

Museum of Finnish Architecture (1996) *Follow the Wood Road.* Press Release. Helsinki.

North Karelia Polytechnic (1996) *Brochure.* Joensuu, Finland.

Organisation for Economic Co-operation and Development (OECD)

(1995) *Reviews of National Policies for Education: Finland: Higher Education.* Paris.

Pulliainen, K. (1987) Reflections on the past, present and future problems of the University of Joensuu, Finland. Paper presented at European Rectors Conference on Strategies for Smaller and Younger Universities, Oulu, Finland, 27–30 Aug. 1987.

University of Joensuu (1993) *Evaluation of the Faculty of Science at the University of Joensuu: Report by the International Evaluation Committee,* 31 Dec. 1993.

(1994a) *Faculty of Education Self-Study Report.*

(1994b) *Faculty of Science Annual Report 1994.*

(1995, 1996) *Faculty of Forestry* (booklets).

Van Vught, F.A. (1989) *Governmental Strategies and Innovation in Higher Education.* Higher Education Policy Series 7. London: Jessica Kingsley.

Chapter 7: The Problem of University Transformation

Carnegie Council on Policy Studies in Higher Education (1980) *Three Thousand Futures.* San Francisco: Jossey-Bass.

Carnegie Foundation for the Advancement of Teaching (1994) *A Classification of Institutions of Higher Education: 1994 Edition.* Princeton, New Jersey.

Clark, B.R. (1983) *The Higher Education System: Academic Organization in Cross-National Perspective.* Berkeley and Los Angeles: University of California Press.

Gibbons, M., Limoges, C., Nowotny, H., Schwartzman, S., Scott, P. and Trow, M. (1994) *The New Production of Knowledge: The Dynanics of Science and Research in Contemporary Societies.* London: Sage Publications.

Henkel, M. (1997) Academic values and the university as corporate enterprise. *Higher Educ. Q.* 51(2): 134–143.

Hölttä, S. (1995) *Towards the Self-Regulative University.* (Publications in Social Sciences No. 23) Joensuu, Finland: University of Joensuu.

Kerr, C. (1993) Universal issues in the development of higher education. In: J.B. Balderston and F.E. Balderston (eds.) *Higher Education in Indonesia: Evolution and Reform.* Berkeley: Center for Studies in Higher Education, University of California, pp. 19–35.

Leonard-Barton, D. (1995) *Wellsprings of Knowledge: Building and Sustaining the Sources of Innovation.* Boston: Harvard Business School Press.

Leslie, D.W. (1996) 'Strategic governance:' the wrong questions? *The Review of Higher Education* 20(1): 101–112.

Leslie, D.W. and Fretwell, Jr. E.K. (1996) *Wise Moves in Hard Times: Creating & Managing Resilient Colleges & Universities.* San Francisco: Jossey-Bass.

Lindblom, C.E. (1959) The science of 'muddling-through.' *Public Admin. Review* 19(2): 78–88.

(1979) Still muddling, not yet through. *Public Admin. Review* 39 Nov./Dec.: 517–526.

MacTaggart, T.J. and Associates (1996) *Restructuring Higher Education: What Works and What Doesn't in Reorganizing Governing Systems.* San Francisco: Jossey-Bass.

Massy, W.F. (1994) *Resource Allocation Reform in the United States.* Washington, D.C.: National Association of College and University Business Officers.

Meek, V.L., Goedegebuure, L., Kivinen, O., and Rinne, R. (eds.) (1996) *The Mockers and Mocked:*

Comparative Perspectives on Differentiation, Convergence and Diversity in Higher Education. Oxford: International Association of Universities Press and Pergamon-Elsevier Science.

Micklethwait, J. and Wooldridge, A. (1996) *The Witch Doctors: Making Sense of the Management Gurus.* New York: Random House (Times Books).

Neave, G. (1996) Homogenization, integration and convergence: the cheshire cat of higher education analysis. In: V.L. Meek, L. Goedegebuure, O. Kivinen, and R. Rinne (eds.) *The Mockers and Mocked: Comparative Perspectives on Differentiation, Convergence and Diversity in Higher Education.* Oxford: International Association of Universities Press and Pergamon-Elsevier Science, pp. 26–41.

Pettigrew, A. and Whipp, R. (1991) *Managing Change for Competitive Success.* Oxford: Blackwell Publishers.

Redner, H. (ed.) (1993) *An Heretical Heir of the Enlightenment: Politics, Policy & Science in the Work of Charles E. Lindblom.* Boulder, Colorado: Westview Press.

Riesman, D. (1973) Commentary and epilogue. In: D. Riesman and V.A. Stadtman (eds.) *Academic Transformation: Seventeen Institutions Under Pressure.* New York: McGraw-Hill.

Scott, P. (1997) The changing role of the university in the production of new knowledge. *Tertiary Education and Management,* 3(1): 5–14.

Shapiro, B.J. and Shapiro, H.T. (1995) Universities in higher education: some problems and challenges in a changing world. Quebec: McGill University (Office of the President, unpublished paper).

Stopford, J.M. and Baden-Fuller, C.W.F. (1994) Creating corporate entrepreneurship. *Strategic Management Journal* 15(7): 521–536.

Teichler, U. (1988) *Changing Patterns of the Higher Education System: The Experience of Three Decades.* London: Jessica Kingsley.

Trow, M.A. (1970) Elite and popular functions in American higher education. In: W.R. Niblett (ed.) *Higher Education: Demand & Response.* San Francisco: Jossey-Bass, pp. 181–201.

Välimaa, J. (1994) A trying game: experiments and reforms in Finnish higher education. *European J. of Educ.* 29(2): 149–163.

Vest, C.M. (1995) Research universities: overextended, underfocused; overstressed, underfunded. Paper presented at the Cornell Symposium on the American University, May 22, 1995. Boston: Massachusetts Institute of Technology (President's Office, unpublished paper).

Williams, G.L. (1995) The 'marketization' of higher education: reforms and potential reforms in higher education finance. In: D.D. Dill and B. Sporn (eds.) *Emerging Patterns of Social Demand and University Reform: Through a Glass Darkly.* Oxford: International Association of Universities and Pergamon-Elsevier Science, pp. 170–193.

Ziman, J. (1994) *Prometheus Bound: Science in a Dynamic Steady State.* Cambridge: Cambridge University Press.

Index